P9-CBW-865

From
Bernice
on Birthday
Dec 5-1946

AS HE SAW IT

ELLIOTT ROOSEVELT

AS HE SAW IT

With a Foreword by Eleanor Roosevelt

DUELL, SLOAN AND PEARCE · *New York*

Second Printing

PRINTED IN THE UNITED STATES OF AMERICA

To all those who believed in my father.

FOREWORD

My husband was always interested in history and always felt that human beings should use the happenings of the present as guides to the future. I know that he would have wanted everyone to write their impressions and their ideas, hoping that each would be valuable in achieving the final objective of a better understanding among the peoples of the world, and the shaping of better tools for keeping the peace.

He had a great deal of family feeling and whenever the opportunity arose, he tried to have what children he could reach, join him. He never would have wanted them had it interfered with their duty and if any one of them felt that something his father wanted was going to interfere with his specific line of duty, my husband always allowed him to express his opinion, and his feeling was the final, deciding factor.

That is one reason why, on so many occasions for short periods of time, he managed to have the children, including his son-in-law and our only daughter, with him when their work or personal obligations did not prevent them from joining him. He wanted their companionship so much that he brought James, our eldest son, to Washington to act as his secretary in spite of the fact that it was pointed out to him that perhaps it was not quite fair to James. He was told that there would be political attacks, and that James' value to his father might be impaired by the mere fact that he was his son. All of these things turned out to be true and eventually James had to give up the relationship, but nevertheless I think that while James was in Washington, my husband took great satisfaction and comfort from his presence and from their work together. Perhaps anyone who has not experienced the loneliness of being the President can not appreciate what having a member of the family near one might mean.

In the family we have always had the habit when any one of us returned from a trip, of trying to dine together on the first night in order that we would hear all the impressions and happenings of the period in which the voyager had been away. We knew only too well that all of us led such very busy lives that if we did not come together immediately, the happenings of the trip would soon recede into the background and be swallowed up by new duties and new occurrences, and we would never catch up with the past.

As I went to none of these history-making trips which are reported in this book, I could only write of things which were told me on those first nights of reunion. But Elliott was there. I remember how excited he was when he came back and now it is doubly interesting to read his more complete account of these highly important days.

Many of the things in this book, I, of course, knew nothing about and had no part in, but I am a great believer in the value of a record which should now be made by every individual who had the opportunity of observing closely any phase of the carrying on of the war and of the plans on which the future organization of the world for peace, were based.

Naturally every human being reports the things which he sees and hears and lives through from his own point of view. Each personality leaves an impression on any situation and that is one reason why accounts of the same facts are so often varied. I am quite sure that many of the people who heard many of the conversations recorded herein, interpreted them differently, according to their own thoughts and beliefs. The records written by all these different individuals are invaluable. This book gives one observer's firsthand account of what went on at the major conferences and will furnish future historians with some of the material which will constitute the final evaluation of history.

—Eleanor Roosevelt

CONTENTS

INTRODUCTION

This will be, only incidentally, a book about the war. It is designed, more importantly, to shed some light on the peace.

The events which I propose to describe in this book, the conversations which I remember, the impressions and the incidents which have formed my present convictions, took place—roughly—from the war's outbreak until shortly after the meeting of the Big Three at Yalta in the Crimea. At the time they took place, let me assure you, I had no intention of writing a book about them. The decision to write this book was taken more recently, and impelled by urgent events. Winston Churchill's speech at Fulton, Missouri, had a hand in this decision; the meetings of the Security Council at Hunter College in New York City and the ideas expressed at those meetings were influential; the growing stockpile of American atom bombs is a compelling factor; all the signs of growing disunity among the leading nations of the world, all the broken promises, all the renascent power politics of greedy and desperate imperialism were my spurs in this undertaking.

The tempo of our times is such that our opinions are not keyed to history but to headlines. Whether we trust or distrust Russia is not conditioned by that nation's mighty contribution to our victory in the war, still the greatest single fact of our lifetime; rather is it molded by scare-print on the front pages of three or four days' newspapers—newspapers often irresponsible in the past, and therefore surely doubly to be doubted in the tremulous present. Our ideas about the loan to Britain are formed not in the long memory of the buzz-bombs that fell on London, nor even in the critical knowledge of continuing British austerity-meals, but in an atmosphere of uncertainty over Britain's imperial intentions. The unity that won the war should be, must be, a fact today, if we are to win the peace. This is simplicity itself: any thinking grade-school student can write a moving and persuasive essay on this theme. But more and more, since V-E Day, and since the atom bomb first fell, this unity has disappeared.

It is because I doubt that we have only *drifted* away from this unity, it is because I am convinced that we are being *shoved* away from it, by men who should know better or—in Walter Lippmann's phrase—"little boys playing with matches," that I felt it important for me to write this book.

Well—and why me? What have I got to offer? After any great world upheaval like this last war, there is bound to be a great spate of books. Generals, ministers, war correspondents, all fly to the typewriter or the not-very-sharp pencil. Nevertheless, for my book I can stake out a small but still quite definite space which is wholly individual.

My qualifications begin with the biological fact of my being my father's son. Like every privilege, this relationship had its drawbacks. I remember his telling me once about these drawbacks—it was in Hyde Park, at a time when he was still Governor of New York, a month or so before his nomination to the Presidency. He was keenly alive to the publicity that attends every action of the children of a man in public life—especially when that man has bitter political enemies. There was, to be sure, little that he could do or wanted to do to control our actions. He took the position that our lives were our own, to do with what we wished and what we could. I imagine that, like any father, he wanted to believe that we would stay out of jail, grow up to be responsible citizens, and be happy, successful people according to our individual lights. But he was careful to give us plenty of rope.

At any rate, taking the rough with the smooth, all the drawbacks of being a President's son must be weighed in the balance against my second qualification for writing this book, which is that it was given to me to be present at and a witness of some of the most important meetings of the war, indeed of our lifetime. Father wanted and needed someone whom he knew well and trusted, a member of his family, if possible, to be with him whenever he was overseas for a wartime conference. This is not to suggest that he didn't know his official advisers well, or that he didn't trust them; but with one of his sons he could wholly relax. He could talk as though he were talking out loud to himself—and he did. Of his sons, I was most often in a position to be drafted as his aide. Thus, when he first met Churchill off Newfoundland, I was attached to a reconnaissance squadron at Gander Lake, Newfoundland; when he came to Casablanca, my outfit was operating out of Algeria; one of our headquarters bases was still in Tunisia when he came to the Near East for the Cairo and Teheran conferences. Only when he went to Yalta was I unable to be at his side.

And, of course, in addition to my hours with him at these meetings, there were times during the war when I came back stateside, once on sick leave, twice on official business, once on leave. Each time I was able to spend some nights at the White House, which meant hours of conversation with him.

As his aide, then, I sat in on most of his appointments, conversations, and conferences—military, political, diplomatic—performing the combined duties of message-taker, errand-runner and note-compiler. In this semi-official capacity I was able to listen to the give-and-take, both formal and informal, of the representatives of all the warring Allies. Churchill, Stalin, Generalissimo and Madame Chiang Kai-shek, the Combined Chiefs of Staff, the commanding generals and admirals in every theater and every branch of the services, Smuts, de Gaulle, Giraud, Hopkins, Robert Murphy, Molotov, the kings of Egypt, Greece, Yugoslavia, and England, emirs and shahs, sultans and princes, premiers, ambassadors, ministers, caliphs, grand viziers—I met them at the door, ushered them in, sat down while they talked with Father —and then listened to his impressions of them, after they had gone.

And when the long conference days were over, and Father had bid his last caller good night, there was hardly an evening that we didn't spend some hours, just the two of us, before he turned out his light to sleep, talking about what had happened that day, comparing notes, pooling impressions. Occasionally he'd question me about what I'd been doing as a photographic reconnaissance officer; more often I'd question him about anything that was troubling me, all the way from what was doing with the Second Front to what did he think of Madame Chiang. He had sufficient confidence in me to tell me the results of his bargaining with Stalin before he had told even his chiefs of staff or his Secretaries of State. Our relationship was one of great good companionship; he had come to like me, I believe, as a respected friend as well as a son.

My opportunities to witness these conferences, then, were on two levels: one as an official Presidential aide, the other as a most intimate friend to the man who was primarily responsible for the unity of the United Nations. It was on this second level that I shared his most intimate thoughts and listened to his most cherished aspirations for the world of peace to follow our military victory. I knew what conditions he predicated for the structure of world peace; I knew what conversations led to them; I knew of the bargains and the promises.

And I have seen the promises violated, and the conditions summarily and cynically disregarded, and the structure of peace disavowed.

That is why I write this book. For my help I have had the official log of the various conferences, which I have supplemented from notes which I took myself, at the time, and from my memory. I have depended more on my notes than on my memory.

I am writing this, then, to you who agree with me that Franklin Roosevelt was the wartime architect of the unity of the United Nations, who agree with me that Franklin Roosevelt's ideals and statesmanship would have been sufficient to keep that unity a vital entity during the postwar period, and who agree with me that the path he charted has been most grievously—and deliberately—forsaken.

I am writing this in the hope that it will be of some service in getting us back on that path. I believe it is possible. I am fearful of the alternative.

AS HE SAW IT

1

TEXAS TO ARGENTIA

The crisis in Europe which was "resolved" by appeasement at Munich, in September of 1938, at the time meant many different things to different people, depending largely on how convinced they were that all humans are citizens of one world. Frankly, the tensity of that weekend as far as I was concerned had almost exclusively selfish motives. I was about to launch a business project, a network of small radio stations in Texas; my worries began and ended with what effects, if any, all the talk of war and the saber-rattling by the Nazis and Fascists would have on my own income and chances for profit.

There's nothing like getting it straight from the source. That September I was in Washington for a few days, and decided to see if I could discreetly pump my father, with an eye to trying to gauge how sure business conditions would be. His second note had just been dispatched to Hitler, and its text released to the press, when I was able to get ten minutes with him alone in his study. I told him about my plans to buy control of the radio stations, and to see if I couldn't make of them a solid, going financial concern.

"Of course," I suggested tentatively, "all this talk about war . . ." And I looked at him expectantly. He pushed his chair back from his desk a bit and looked right back at me. There was a pause. I began again, a little lamely, "Read the headlines in the papers, you figure it's all going to start first thing tomorrow. Won't do new business enterprises any good, I guess."

He grinned. "What do you want me to tell you? That there won't be war? That you should go ahead with your radio project? That nobody need worry? That you're sure to make a profit the first year, and be rich by the end of the third?"

"I thought maybe . . ."

"I'll tell you what I know, which is only about what anybody else knows, who has his eyes open. Sooner or later there'll be a showdown in Europe. Sooner or later Britain and France will decide Hitler's gone too far. It doesn't look as though it'll be this weekend, but even that you can't be too sure about. Russia's rôle . . . the Czechoslovak people . . ."

"But just because there's a showdown in Europe doesn't necessarily mean that *we'll* have to get involved?"

"We're all working hard to see that that's the case. We're all as anxious as the dickens to make sure we stay out. We all have the highest hopes, the *highest* hopes." He paused for a moment, and fussed with a gadget on his desk, frowning abstractedly. "Look," he said suddenly, "in your place, I'd go ahead on your radio project as fast and hard as I could. You've no reason to give it up because of a few newspaper headlines. Get on the ball and keep on it. I'm sure you'll do well."

That was that. On my way home to Texas, I tried to figure out that sudden, almost too-confident assurance, and wondered if there were anything between the lines, so to speak. But September and October of 1938 were still months when most of us Americans were several hundred light-years from reality; eventually I shrugged my shoulders, decided I should forget about Europe and get to work in Texas. Which I did.

If more of us—and I certainly include myself in this group—had done a little less shoulder-shrugging and paid a little more attention to what was going on just around the corner in Manchuria or Czechoslovakia, it would have paid us dividends and saved us blood. Just to make sure how accurate a truism this is, I looked back over some of the official papers of those days, and even earlier. Here, for instance, are the notes of a press conference that Father held on April 20, 1938. A skeptical reporter is questioning him about the need for military defenses in the Pacific. The reporter suggests that we will never be able to defend the Philippines and our other Pacific islands while simultaneously ensuring our own Western Hemisphere against attack. And Father answers:

"Well, of course, if you have only one enemy, then you're all right. But suppose there are two enemies, from two different places. Then you would have to be a bit shifty on your feet. You have to lick one of them first and then bring your military forces around and then lick the other. That is about your only chance."

And so, while the Great Debate began that was to engross the country in the months before Pearl Harbor, Father was doing all he could to make sure that any Pearl Harbors would not find us unprepared. In Congress, Brewster of Maine, Ham Fish of New York, Vandenberg of Michigan, Capper of Kansas, and Borah of Idaho were leading the opposition to any adequate military or naval appropriations bills; the Hearst papers and the McCormick-Patterson axis were denouncing collective security and calling for isolation.

In June of 1940 I was in New York on business. When I stopped over in Washington on my way back to Texas, one of the things I had on my mind was what any businessman would have found to worry about. Taxes. Especially that excess profits tax. Big business could handle it all right, but for a small business, capitalized at low figures and with a considerable outstanding debt, it made rocky going. I got talking with Father about that one just as he was finishing breakfast, before the day's work.

"How about it, Pop? Doesn't the Government want to see us little fellows able to pay off debts and get in the black?"

He grinned and pushed the litter of Chicago, New York, and Washington newspapers to the floor. "You had coffee?" he asked.

"Never mind the coffee. What about this excess profits tax?"

"You don't think your company is typical, do you?"

"No, but . . ."

"And you'll grant that the money has got to be raised?

And that now that these large corporations are beginning to work under defense contracts, cost-plus contracts, that their soaring profits make as good a place as any to find the money? And that we've got to have the money, if we're to build an adequate navy and army and air force?"

"All that, sure. But how about my little—"

He interrupted me. "There's no question that a tax law will work hardship on somebody. No matter what the tax law. Ordinarily, I'm more anxious than the next fellow to see that the little businessman gets the edge in competition over the big man. But business and taxes aren't our only problem right now. Right now the problems are a lot bigger. A *whale* of a lot bigger. I'm sorry about your own headaches. Here—have some aspirin."

I laughed.

Well, there *was* one other problem on my mind. "What about conscription?" I asked him.

It was such an abrupt question that at first he thought I meant conscription of corporate profits. Then, "Oh. You mean the draft. What about it?"

"Well, I just wondered what you felt John and Franklin and I should do, if and when the draft bill is passed. I guess Jimmy is a little old to . . ."

"In any case, Jimmy's already in the Marine Corps Reserve," he reminded me.

"Is there any indication of what sort of draft bill will be passed? I mean, age limits, that sort of thing?"

"I want to make one thing very clear. If the draft bill becomes law, it'll be a matter for each of you to wrestle out with your own conscience. If you want to wait until the draft becomes a fact—if it ever does—then that's up to each of you, too. If the draft becomes law, then each of you'll have a local draft board, and the draft board will take suitable action.

"As for my giving you any advice as to how you should act, what you should do, you ought to know me better than that. Your business has always been your business. An act establishing a draft of able-bodied men won't change that. Nothing will."

And that was that.

From my standpoint, it wasn't too satisfactory an interview. I knew, if anything, less than I had when I'd gone in. He hadn't been optimistic about the tax problems confronting small business; he hadn't indicated in any way what he thought would be a sensible course of action for me personally. I say the interview was unsatisfactory, because that's how I felt at the time. Looking back now, engaging in a little Sunday quarterbacking, I realize that he did just right in always contriving that I should make up my own mind.

Back at work in Texas that summer, I made up my mind fairly quickly. Texas is a good place to be in, when it comes to making up your mind about volunteering for your country's army or navy. In Texas, it's the thing to do. And I had to admit, reading my newspapers soberly, morning after morning, that it certainly was beginning to look as though sooner or later our country would be forced into the war. My business? It was holding its own; actually, any rise in production because of war orders would probably mean increased advertising revenue. Anything to keep me from joining up? I couldn't see what. And after all, what was I committing myself to? Only a year's military training. (Well, that's what *I* thought.) Why not join up? At least it wouldn't do any harm to find out more about it.

So in August I was back again in Washington, at the War Department.

Some years before I'd been a private pilot; I'd worked in the aviation industry; I'd been an aviation editor for the Hearst papers; so I figured the Army Air Forces were for me. In a sense, this was Roosevelt disloyalty to the Navy, but it must be remembered that I'm the Roosevelt who didn't go to Harvard.

I'd known "Hap" Arnold when he was a lieutenant colonel, stationed out at March Field in California, years before. Father had a high regard for Hap's ability and his ideas; by 1940 Arnold was a major general and commander of the Army Air Forces. It was logical for me to drop in to say hello to him, and find out from some officer on his staff what I could do about joining up. As a pilot, I hoped.

But as a pilot, it was no go. The physical they gave me was enough: they told me I was definitely unfit for combat service, that I'd have to sign waivers even to get an administrative job. I grabbed at that chance; the officers I talked to thought my experience as a radio network executive would be valuable in the procurement division; and my age at the time qualified me for a reserve commission as captain—that part of it was routine. All this I'd kept quiet about; never told any of my family. Then on September 19th I was notified my commission had been put through. I was ready to tell my father.

At the White House, Father had a series of appointments with his Cabinet members. I wangled my way in between two of them.

"Look, Pop."

He glanced at the piece of paper with my orders on it and looked up with tears in his eyes. I was the first of his sons to volunteer. He couldn't speak for a moment. Then, "I'm very proud of you."

His emotion made me pretty proud, myself.

That weekend nearly the whole family was at Hyde Park to celebrate a pair of birthdays: my grandmother's, which fell on the twenty-first, and mine, which is on the twenty-third. We had a joint party, and that evening, at dinner, Father lifted his glass and proposed a toast:

"To Elliott. He's the first of the family to think seriously enough, and soberly enough, about the threat to America to join his country's armed forces. We're all very proud of him. I'm the proudest."

And he and my mother and grandmother and brothers drank to me.

In many ways, I have since felt that my closeness to my father dated from that moment in his office in the executive wing of the White House when I showed him my notification of commission. Of course, there had been the summer when he and I went to Europe, just the two of us, the summer of my twenty-first birthday. But this was different. From this moment on he would talk far more intimately, with far more confidence and far closer bonds. It was as though he had mentally—without ever telling me—set me a test, and I had come through. It meant a great deal to him, and I assure you it meant a great deal to me, too.

That night, in his bedroom, when I'd come in to say good night, he asked me to stick around and chat for a few minutes. He asked me how it felt, and I told him: Fine; we talked idly for a few minutes about Wright Field, in Dayton, Ohio, to which I'd been assigned. He asked me how I felt about the war. The only doubt that there'd been in my mind was one which was in a lot of minds those days: How come we were shipping scrap iron to Japan? Surely we knew that scrap iron to Japan meant dead Chinese. . . .

"We're a nation of peace," he answered, thoughtfully. "That's more than just a condition, it's a frame of mind. It means that we're not looking for war; it means we don't want war; it means we're not prepared for war. Scrap iron—don't laugh—scrap iron is not classified as war matériel. So Japan or any other country with which we have commercial contacts is perfectly at liberty to buy our scrap iron."

"But . . ."

"Even more. If we were suddenly to stop our sales of scrap iron to Japan, she would be within her rights in considering that we had performed an unfriendly act, that we were choking off and starving her commercially.

"Even more. She'd be entitled to consider such an action on our part sufficient cause to break off diplomatic relations with us.

"I'll go even further. If she thought we were sufficiently unprepared for war, sufficiently unarmed, she might even use it as an excuse to declare war."

"She'd be bluffing."

"Maybe. Even probably. But are we in a position to call her bluff?"

I was thinking of the editorials in Colonel McCormick's Chicago *Tribune,* and of the speeches made by a handful of senators and representatives, that Japan had no warlike intentions toward us, that there was no threat to our interests in the Far East. I was thinking about the criticism that had been leveled at Father for warmongering.

"We are, in essence and in fact," he went on, "appeasing Japan. It's an ugly word, and don't think I like it. But it's what we're doing. We're appeasing Japan in order to gain the time we have to have to build a first-rate navy, a first-rate army . . ."

"And a first-rate air force," I put in.

"And a first-rate air force." He smiled. "That's right: I'll have to remember to talk air force more often, around you."

A few days later I was off to my new, strange work as a captain in the procurement division of the Army Air Forces. To be honest, the thought had never occurred to me that Father's enemies would try to make political capital out of what for me was a genuine act, my volunteering and applying for a commission. I hadn't joined up for fun, or because I thought the life would be more pleasant than carrying on my business in Texas.

I'd have been a fool if I had thought that. But in the next few weeks—wham!

During the Presidential campaign of 1940 I got some thirty-five thousand letters and postcards, from all over the country, most of them unsigned, of course.

At the time, you may be sure, those letters and postcards rankled. Father's swing through the Midwest in October brought him to Dayton at about the time when these letters and postcards were raining in on me, a thousand in every mail; he planned to take advantage of his itinerary to stop off for an inspection of Wright Field accompanied by General Hap Arnold; so I made up my mind to see him for a few minutes in the private car of his campaign train.

"Believe it or not, Pop, it's not so much for me. But things like this aren't doing your chances any good."

He looked serious. After all, the accusations that I'd been trying to dodge combat with this desk job, and that he was using his influence to keep me from danger aren't the sort that are lightly made nor lightly received. He asked me what I could do about it, what I intended to do about it.

"I'd like to resign. Resign my commission. I wanted to tell you about it, because I know how you felt when I told you . . ."

"You talking to me now as Commander-in-Chief?" His eyes twinkled.

"If you want. Sure."

"Hold on a minute." Then, turning to Steve Early, "Ask Hap Arnold to step back for a second, will you, Steve?"

When General Arnold came back to the lounge, Father told him what I'd asked. "I'm going to leave this one up to you, Hap," he said. "It's your problem. Do with it what you want." And he turned away, to the window.

General Arnold cocked an eye at me. "You serious, Captain?"

"I certainly am, sir."

"What do you want to do? Re-enlist as a private? That it?"

"I'd thought of the RCAF, sir, if I can't re-enlist as a private."

"Mmm. Well, put your request for resignation through official channels. Give all your reasons. It'll be acted on."

And so up through official channels went my official request. And a week later, back down through the same channels came the answer: Request rejected. I then started a systematic bombardment of my superior officers to get a change of assignment which would wangle me some sort of overseas duty. Before too long, I got results. I was transferred to Bolling Field, to take a training course as an air intelligence officer, under a hardworking, clear-thinking young West Pointer named Lauris Norstad. As soon as I completed the intelligence course, I was assigned to the Twenty-First Reconnaissance Squadron under command of Major Jimmy Crabb. The Twenty-First was stationed in Newfoundland, doing patrol work in the North Atlantic against the Nazi submarine threat to our shipping. I wasn't all the way overseas yet, but I felt that I was on the way, at least

I've reached around in my mind for the proper word to describe conditions—weather conditions, living conditions, conditions of terrain or rather lack-of-terrain—up in Newfoundland, in March of 1941. Perhaps "rugged" will serve, if by "rugged" you will understand that I mean miserable, muddy, bleak, and woebegone, all rolled into one. Operating as much as anything on the theory that nothing could be more unpleasant than Newfoundland in March of 1941, I volunteered for a survey job to locate air-force sites in the North Arctic area which could be used as staging points for the delivery of fighter aircraft from the United States to the United Kingdom. The most ticklish aspect of this undertaking was to keep the Army from rubbing rough against the Navy; and the job took me from Labrador to Baffin Island to Greenland and Iceland and eventually clear over to England, where I was to compare findings with British fliers and officials of the Air Ministry. I would have preferred, frankly, to have timed my visit to England a bit later: I arrived at the tail-end of the Nazis' May-June blitz of 1941. To be sure, it was only the tail-end, but it was enough. I shared with everybody else who experienced it the shock of seeing the ruined buildings, and the helplessness of immobility while bombs dropped on all sides.

During that first wartime trip to Britain I was invited for one brief weekend to Chequers, the Prime Minister's country home. It was a pleasant sort of family weekend, with two moments of embarrassment: the first when a British butler right out of an M-G-M movie met me at the door and inquired after my luggage, and all I had to offer for his inspection was a comb and a toothbrush;

the other when, after having been lent a handsome set of Chinese-silk pajamas, presumably the property of my host, I awoke Sunday morning to find that, since they'd been rather too small, I'd split them from stem to stern.

By midsummer of 1941, my squadron had located five sites for stations in the Arctic Circle. We gave them names familiar probably only to the fliers that were to use them in the next four years. Goose Bay in Labrador, Bluie East on Greenland, and Crystal One in Quebec, Crystal Two and Crystal Three on Baffin Island were our contributions to the ferry system that enabled so many fighter and bomber planes to get over to England in the summers of '42 and '43.

By early August I was back at Baffin Island, slogging through knee-deep tundra, surveying a possible airport site at the head of Cumberland Sound, when an order was radioed through that I should return at once to my base at Newfoundland. Routine, I figured. At my base at Gander Lake I was assigned an OA-10 Grumman and a pilot. We were told we were to pick up the general commanding American forces on Newfoundland at St. John's on Friday, August 8th, and then proceed to the naval base at Argentia. Hmmm. All I could do was speculate that some brass or other wanted to confer about the bases I was surveying.

Our commanding general was sitting silent in the back of our little Grumman, I in the co-pilot seat, when we cleared the mountain spur overlooking the harbor at Argentia. The pilot whistled. The bay was filled with warships, and a lot of them were big, too. We looked at each other, frowning with perplexity. Our radio was issuing instructions as to which mooring-post we should tie to, and how long a wait we would have for a tender. Meantime we were still trying to dope out this flotilla of cruisers and destroyers riding at anchor. The only sense we could make of it was that we had happened in on an Atlantic maneuver.

A few minutes later I got the answer, when, after a tender had whisked us to a cruiser that turned out to be the *Augusta,* we were piped over the side, and there, in back of the cruiser's captain, I saw Brigadier General "Pa" Watson, Father's military aide, and Vice Admiral Wilson Brown, his naval aide. I was so astonished to see them, trying so hard to put two and two together, that I almost forgot a bit of naval etiquette that I'd been taught in the days when I was a child and Father was Assistant Secretary of the Navy. Pa Watson grinned, Admiral Brown waved, and just in time I remembered, and turned toward the cruiser's stern to salute the American flag. Then Pa was shaking my hand and murmuring about how "the Commander-in-Chief would like to see you." I started forward, and ran into my brother Franklin Junior, at that time a lieutenant (jg) in the Navy.

"Hey! You too?"

"All I knew was that the *Mayrant* was ordered off convoy duty with another destroyer last week. Told us we were to patrol as part of the screen force guarding the entrance to the harbor. Then this morning they said I should report to the Commander-in-Chief aboard the *Augusta.*" He ran his finger inside his collar. "I was trying to figure what the hell had I done so terrible that Admiral King'd want to haul me up on the carpet."

"Where's Pop?"

"For'ard. In the captain's quarters. What'd *you* think?"

"Same as you, I guess. That this was some sort of naval maneuver."

"Come this way. Hope you brought yourself a change of clothes."

"I didn't. Why?"

"Looks like we're going to be here two or three days, anyway."

That was Friday, just before lunch. I had only the shirt under my tunic, and I wasn't to leave till the following Tuesday. Fortunately, Father's neck-size and mine were about the same. You'll agree that it wouldn't have been appropriate to witness the signing of the Atlantic Charter in a dirty shirt.

2

THE ATLANTIC CHARTER

Franklin and I got in to see Father for a few minutes before lunch on Friday. We didn't have more than a chance to say hello and find out how Mother and the rest of the family were before:

"Here," he said. "I got Pa Watson to bring this up for you," and he handed me a military *aiguillette* of aide to the Commander-in-Chief. "For the next few days only," he smiled, and gave Franklin a naval counterpart of mine.

"You look wonderful, Pop. But how come all this? You on a fishing trip?"

Father roared with laughter. "That's what the newspapers think. They think I'm fishing somewhere off the Bay of Fundy." He was as delighted as a kid, boasting of how he had thrown the newspapermen off the scent by going as far as Augusta, Maine, on the presidential yacht *Potomac*. Then he told us what it was all about.

"I'm meeting Churchill here. He's due in tomorrow on the *Prince of Wales*. Harry Hopkins is with him."

And he leaned back to watch the effect of his announcement on us. I guess it was big. I wasn't near any mirrors, but he enjoyed it.

I don't want to pursue this story any further without a word about the White House correspondents whom Father had left behind. He did it because he had made an agreement with Churchill that there should be no newspaper coverage of this first meeting, either by reporters or cameramen. After that, in carrying out his part of the bargain, he enjoyed himself thoroughly, giving the press the slip, much as a twelve-year-old boy playing cops-and-robbers will enjoy shaking a playmate who is trying to "shadow" him. But when Churchill arrived, next day, he arrived complete with press retinue, not very well disguised as Ministry of Information officials. It was the first time that Churchill surprised Father in this way. It was not the last.

As for the fishing, Father in fact did fish, once. It was the day before I got there. He caught a What-Is-It, unidentifiable by anyone on board. "Have it sent to the Smithsonian," Father suggested, and tried no more fishing during the whole trip.

There were many reasons why it had been planned that this first wartime meeting of Father with Churchill should take place where it did. Security dictated meeting outside of Washington; if it had been Washington, the gossip and the rumors would have dwarfed any possible final results. Both Father and the Prime Minister were naval men; it was in that capacity that they had last met, in 1919; the idea of a meeting at sea was guaranteed to intrigue the imagination of each of them. But clearly they could not meet in the open sea; the danger of Nazi submarine action made it impossible. Where then? Some well-protected harbor on a sparsely settled coastline or at some Atlantic island. The Azores? Portuguese; out of the question. Personally I would have chosen Bermuda, or one of the West Indies; even in August Newfoundland is bleak and cold; fog settles a good bit of the time; the sun is a stranger. But Newfoundland had apparent advantages, too: not too heavily settled, plenty of British and Canadian and American troops stationed near by, and—best of all—any concentration of warships in the harbor of Argentia would cause no speculation inasmuch as our Navy was already engaged in building it up as a base.

So here I was at Argentia, and looking forward to the few days of change from routine duty, too.

That day at lunch, and during the cold, gray afternoon that followed, Father and I lazed around his quarters, catching up on family news. For a time Franklin was with us, telling us about his destroyer's convoy duty to Iceland. Father looked well, and was obviously enjoying his break in routine. He asked me about my work up above the Arctic Circle, and even more about the trip to England, what it had been like, the temper of the people I'd talked to, what it was like being blitzed (I'd had only a few days of it, and was hardly qualified to testify), what I thought of Churchill, whom he had not seen in some years, and so on. I asked him what was the purpose of this meeting he was about to have.

"*You* were there," he answered. "*You* saw the people. You've even told me how they look—gray and thin and strained. A meeting like this one will do a world of good for British morale. Won't it?"

I nodded.

"The Nazis are riding high, these days. Masters of Europe. I don't imagine there are many Americans left by now who don't agree that we've got to lend Britain at least moral aid, or find ourselves facing the guns and the bombs."

"For morale, then," I prompted.

"For more than that. What about our Lend-Lease schedules? The British know they're at their production limits—and that those limits don't include an offensive war. This meeting is to work out production schedules, and—what's more important to the British—delivery schedules." I lighted his cigarette. "They'll be worried about how much of our production we're going to divert to the Russians."

"And?"

"I know already how much faith the P.M. has in Russia's ability to stay in the war." He snapped his fingers to indicate zero.

"I take it you have more faith than that."

"Harry Hopkins has more. He's able to convince me."

Of course, at the time we were talking, American war production was still just a trickle. The British were fearful lest what they got would turn out to be just half-a-trickle.

"The P.M. is coming here tomorrow because—although I doubt that he'll show it—he knows that without America, England can't stay in the war."

I whistled. I'd seen the tail end of the May blitz, which

blanketed most British industrial centers, but I hadn't realized their plight was as serious as all that. And with the Russians retreating steadily back across the steppes . . .

"Of course," my father went on, "Churchill's greatest concern is how soon will we be in the war. He knows very well that so long as American effort is confined to production, it will do no more than keep England in. He knows that to mount an offensive, he needs American troops." Abruptly he asked, "Did you read the English papers while you were in London?"

I mentioned that I'd noticed a number of articles in English papers which had taken the United States severely to task, alleging that we were interested only in seeing Britain bled white before we came in at the sixtieth second to save the day. Father nodded triumphantly.

"Watch and see," he said. "Watch and see if the P.M. doesn't start off by demanding that we immediately declare war against the Nazis."

I wasn't quite clear on what we had to gain from this meeting. "Aside, of course, from our being on Britain's side already, morally."

"There's that," Father said, "and it's important. And you mustn't forget that our chiefs of staff are here with me, too. There's a lot they can learn. What's the exact status of British war potential? Is it true that they've reached the absolute bottom of the barrel, as far as manpower's concerned?"

"Who's here?" I asked. I'd seen only Father and his aides.

"King, Stark, Marshall, Arnold . . . plenty of brass. You'll see 'em."

A courier came in with a bag full of official mail, interrupting us for a few minutes. When he had gone, Father returned to the background of the meeting. I think he was really in a way rehearsing himself for the conversations he was to begin next day, running over the various underlying reasons for his being there, priming himself for Churchill's requests.

"Another thing," he said. "The British Empire is at stake here. It's something that's not generally known, but British bankers and German bankers have had world trade pretty well sewn up in their pockets for a long time. Despite the fact that Germany lost, in the last war. Well, now, that's not so good for American trade, is it?" He cocked an eyebrow at me. "If in the past German and British economic interests have operated to exclude us from world trade, kept our merchant shipping down, closed us out of this or that market, and now Germany and Britain are at war, what should we do?

"One thing we know right off. That is, we can't afford to be greedy, and pick sides only from the standpoint of what will profit us most greatly. Leaving to one side for the moment the fact that Nazism is hateful, and that our natural interests, our *hearts*, are with the British. But there's another angle. We've got to make clear to the British from the very outset that we don't intend to be simply a good-time Charlie who can be used to help the British Empire out of a tight spot, and then be forgotten forever."

"I don't see exactly what you're driving at," I put in.

"Churchill told me that he was not his Majesty's Prime Minister for the purpose of presiding over the dissolution of the British Empire. [Churchill later repeated this in a radio address.] I think I speak as America's President when I say that America won't help England in this war simply so that she will be able to continue to ride roughshod over colonial peoples." He paused.

"I think," I said carefully, "that I can see there will be a little fur flying here and there, in the next few days."

"We'll see," said my father. "We'll see."

That afternoon, about four-thirty, Sumner Welles and Averell Harriman came aboard the *Augusta*. They had papers to go over with Father, so I left until shortly before dinnertime. Conversation at dinner was almost exclusively small talk. We all turned in early.

Before nine o'clock Saturday morning we were all on deck to watch the *Prince of Wales* slide in and drop anchor not far from the *Augusta*. I was holding Father's arm. We thought we saw a party of people which might include Churchill on the deck of the British man-of-war, but it was again a gray, drizzly morning, and you couldn't be sure.

A couple of hours later, the P.M. came aboard, with the principal members of his staff. It was the first time the two had seen each other since 1919, but it didn't take them long, talking about their correspondence, their transatlantic phone conversations, their health, their jobs and their worries, to be calling each other "Franklin" and "Winston." Those names were for private, of course; when other officials were present, it was

"Mr. President" and "Mr. Prime Minister." Eventually, Father gave up this pretense at formality, although Churchill was always to adhere punctiliously to it.

Today, this first visit was purely protocol; the P.M. had a letter from his King to present to Father. More notable was the staff of advisers accompanying Churchill. In contrast to the small party Father brought along to the conference, Churchill—well, he didn't have everybody from A to Z, but he had everybody from Beaverbrook to Yool. It was at this time that we learned there were Ministry of Information officials present, complete with notebooks and cameras. General Hap Arnold slipped up in back of me, to whisper in my ear that we'd damn well better get some cameramen and some film aboard in a hurry, and did I know if there were any air-force cameramen available up at Gander Lake? That morning I sent our pilot back in the Grumman, to get supplies and a couple of Army photographers, so that our press would have at least some service on the conference.

As a matter of fact, the wealth of British advisers, aides, braid, and brass was somewhat embarrassing to Hap Arnold in another connection, too. He was to find that he was at a disadvantage, in the staff conferences that followed, because he had no assistant, while his British counterpart was three-deep in secretaries, aides, and what-nots. So at one or two sessions, I was pressed into service as note-taker for the Army Air Forces.

At lunch, on this first day of their meeting, Father and the P.M. were alone with Harry Hopkins, who had come over on the *Prince of Wales* with Churchill. It was good to see Harry again, and good to see him looking relatively well. I'd had a small hand in his better health; on his way to London, the month before, he'd stopped over at Gander Lake, and we'd taken him for a day's fishing. Real fishing: for rainbow trout, with dry fly. In one day Harry seemed to shed ten years of age. Now he was back again at the job, faithful and hardworking.

The rest of our party lunched buffet as Admiral King's guests. I joined Father and the P.M. in the captain's cabin after lunch: they were sitting opposite each other, politely sparring.

"My information, Franklin, is that the temper of the American people is strongly in our favor. That in fact they are ready to join the issue."

"You can find counter-indications," drily.

"But the debate on Lend-Lease . . ."

"If you are deeply interested in American opinion, I recommend you read the Congressional Record, every day, Winston."

Two ideas were clashing head-on: the P.M. clearly was motivated by one governing thought, that we should declare war on Nazi Germany straightaway; the President was thinking of public opinion, American politics, all the intangibles that lead to action and at once betray it. At length, after draining his glass, the P.M. heaved himself to his feet. It was close on two-thirty. Father mentioned that he was sending, on behalf of our Navy, gifts to the officers and men of the *Prince of Wales* and her three escorting destroyers. The P.M. acknowledged this information with a nod and a short word, and left.

That afternoon, the nineteen hundred and fifty gift-boxes, containing cigarettes, fresh fruit, and cheese, were passed out to the British seamen. And that afternoon the chiefs of staff worked over their agenda: production, priorities, shipping, war potentials—matériel, men, and money—the three musts of modern war. For a time I assisted Hap Arnold at this conference; later, after our meeting was over, I was lighting a cigarette for an American Navy officer.

"Love us!" he murmured, as we started out toward the main deck. "All they want is our birthright!"

What he said was true; and yet at the same time it was difficult to remain objective, having seen, as I had, the character of the fight the British were putting up, and the length of the odds against them.

There was a formal dinner in the captain's saloon of the *Augusta* that Saturday night. Father was host. The P.M., of course, sat at his right, and the others included Cadogan, Britain's Permanent Under-Secretary of State for Foreign Affairs; Lord Cherwell, aide to the P.M.; Sumner Welles; Harry Hopkins; Averell Harriman; and the American and British chiefs of staff. At dinner, and afterwards, too, as the evening wore on toward midnight, I saw Father in a new rôle. My experience of him in the past had been that he dominated every gathering he was part of; not because he insisted on it so much as that it always seemed his natural due. But not tonight. Tonight Father listened. Somebody else was holding the audience, holding it with grand, rolling, periodic speeches, never quite too florid, always ripe and fruity to the point where it seemed you'd be able to take his sentences in your hands and squeeze them until the juice ran out.

Winston Churchill held every one of us, that night—and was conscious every second of the time that he *was* holding us. All that Father did was to throw in an occasional question—just drawing him on, drawing him out. Harry, too, made an occasional comment, but only when the P.M. was pausing for breath. By and large, all of us who were in uniform were silent, only occasionally whispering an aside to each other: "Match?" "Thanks." "Pass me the water pitcher, hunh?" "Ssshhh!" "Lot of vinegar in him, hmmm?" "Yeah—and that ain't all!"

Churchill rared back in his chair, he slewed his cigar around from cheek to cheek and always at a jaunty angle, he hunched his shoulders forward like a bull, his hands slashed the air expressively, his eyes flashed. He held the floor that evening and he talked. Nor were the rest of us silent because we were bored. He held us enthralled even when we were inclined to disagree with him.

He told of the course of the war. He told of battle after battle, lost: "But Britain always wins the wars!" He told us with a fair show of frankness just how close to defeat his countrymen had actually come: ". . . but Hitler and his generals were too stupid. They never knew. Or else they never dared." For a time his talk was colored over with an insistent note of pleading: "It's your only chance! You've *got* to come in beside us! If you don't declare war, declare war, I say, without waiting for them to strike the first blow, they'll strike it after we've gone under, and their first blow will be their last as well!" But even while his listeners could detect the underlying appeal, his whole bearing gave the impression of an indomitable force that would do all right, thank you, even if we didn't heed his warning.

And every now and then, Father would throw in a question:

"The Russians?"

"The Russians!" There was an edge of contempt in his voice, and then he seemed almost to catch himself. "Of course, they're much stronger than we ever dared to hope. But no one can tell how much longer . . ."

"Then you don't think they'll be able to hold out?"

"When Moscow falls . . . As soon as the Germans are beyond the Caucasus . . . When Russian resistance finally ceases . . ."

Always his answers were definite, unconditional. There were no "ifs," there was little or no credence put in Russian resistance. He had the dice in his hand, that August night, and he was casting for heavy stakes. He was anxious to make clear to us that the lion's share of Lend-Lease should go to the British lion; that any aid to the Soviets was simply to temporize, and eventually to lose, but surely; and that led him all the more certainly to his one final conclusion:

"The Americans *must* come in at our side! You must come in, if you are to survive!"

And Father listened, intently, seriously, now and then rubbing his eyes, fiddling with his pince-nez, doodling on the tablecloth with a burnt match. But never an aye, nay, or maybe, came from the Americans sitting around that smoke-filled saloon.

It was like a second round, between friendly adversaries. It came to no decision, but there was nobody in the crowd who felt like yelling for a better scrap. All of us wanted both to win.

Sunday morning, just before we were to leave the *Augusta* for a church service on the quarterdeck of the *Prince of Wales,* I got a message that our Grumman had landed not long since, with two Army Air Forces photographers aboard her, laden with still and moving-picture film. I gave Hap Arnold the word, and they came along with the President's party.

It was a bit after eleven in the morning when we were piped aboard the British warship. Overhead, the clouds, which had been resolutely leaden and wet for the past week, were beginning to break, almost as though by signal.

The sun broke through.

Arrayed around the quarterdeck was the British ship's company; beside them were two hundred and fifty of our sailors and marines as well. The ship's pulpit had been draped with the American and British colors.

We sang *O God, Our Help in Ages Past,* and *Onward, Christian Soldiers,* and *Eternal Father, Strong to Save,* our voices lifting up and out over the waters of the bay strongly and warmly. We prayed in unison.

I don't know what the others there were thinking, but I was thinking: Here, on this deck, with the light of the occasional sun on them, are a couple of men who are important only as they stand at the head of two mighty nations. And thinking about that, I thought of the millions in Britain working and going without, producing bombs by day and lying sleepless under bombs by night. I thought of her armies, pushed back but grim; men in slacks and shorts and kilts; men with a new flash on their shoulders, one that read COMMANDO; men in RAF blue and brown, drawn and edgy; the men and officers of this very ship I stood on, who had fought long and wearily, who regarded this trip as a heaven-sent rest, and who, poor fellows, were fated to go down with this very same ship a few months later, stabbed by Japanese torpedoes.

And I thought how at home, in America, factories were coming to life; women from the kitchens and boys from the farm were beginning to learn new and exciting and important trades, millions upon millions of them; everybody was touched in some way by the war: if they weren't in the armed forces or in a war plant, then they were prowling the streets at night in an air-raid warden's helmet, feeling a little foolish, maybe, but part of their country, nonetheless; everybody part of a mighty effort, a transcending effort.

If Britain was breathless a bit, groggy under a continuing series of punches, America was beginning to flex a hell of a set of muscles.

And here stood their leaders, praying, *Our Father, Which art in Heaven, hallowed be Thy name. . . .*

Then we were at lunch, guests of the P.M. And there was the moment when someone rapped for quiet and cried out: "Gentlemen, the King!" and there was a great scraping back of chairs and shuffling of feet and a moment of silence while the glasses were lifted up and then the wine sipped. This was pomp, and perhaps the opportunity for cynicism at the same time, but it was undeniably impressive, too. At least for me, who had never witnessed it before.

On our way back to the *Augusta,* to begin the military sessions which were to go on all afternoon, I said to Father some of the things which had been on my mind at church service that morning.

"It was our keynote," he said. "If nothing else had happened while we were here, that would have cemented us. 'Onward, Christian Soldiers.' We *are,* and we *will* go on, with God's help."

The afternoon sessions, at which the military opposites got together, were the occasion for something of a breakdown from the ideal unity of the morning. Britain's advocates were again hard at it, trying to convince us to divert more and more and more Lend-Lease supplies to the United Kingdom, and less and less and less to the Soviet Union. I don't believe their motives were directly political, although it must be agreed that, underneath, their lack of confidence in Russia's staying-power was itself political. In these conversations, Marshall and King and Arnold continued insistent that there was logic in giving the Soviets all the help that could be spared. After all, our line of reasoning ran, the German armies were in Russia; tanks and planes and guns in the hands of the Soviets would mean dead Nazis; all that Lend-Lease would accomplish in Britain, for the moment, would be to build up stockpiles. Nor could we afford, of course, to forget our own defense needs, what was required to build up our own Army and Navy.

Admiral Pound, General Dill, Air Chief Marshal Freeman—these three rang every change on the argument that the stockpiles, in the long run, would prove of more value to the overall Allied war effort. They hammered at the concept that war matériel to the Soviets was destined just to be war matériel captured by the Nazis, that American self-interest dictated a channeling of the bulk of supplies into England. Fortunately, the American spokesmen saw America's self-interest—and the broad interests of the war effort—in a different light. For myself, I was wondering whether it was the British Empire's purpose to see the Nazis and the Russians cancel each other out, while Britain grew strong.

Meantime, Father was going over a draft of some notes with Sumner Welles. At this stage, we weren't sure what it was about: actually, of course, what they were working on was the Atlantic Charter, and the note to Stalin expressing our common determination for a common, mutual victory over Hitlerism.

The P.M. returned to the *Augusta* for dinner that night. This occasion was more intimate: the brass and the braid had departed. It was Father and the P.M., their immediate aides, and Franklin Junior and I. And therefore it was much more of an opportunity to get to know Churchill.

Once again, he was in fine form. The cigars were burned to ashes, the brandy disappeared steadily. But there was no marked change. If anything, his mind seemed to work more clearly, and his tongue more easily.

But there *was* a change, from the talk of a night before. Last night, Churchill had talked without interruption, except for questions. Tonight, there were other men's thoughts being tossed into the kettle, and the kettle correspondingly began to bubble up and—once or twice—nearly over. You sensed that two men accustomed to leadership had sparred, had felt each other out, and were now readying themselves for outright challenge, each of the other. It must be remembered that at this time Churchill was the war leader, Father only the president of a state which had indicated its sympathies in a tangible fashion. Thus, Churchill still arrogated the conversational lead, still dominated the after-dinner hours. But the difference was beginning to be felt.

And it was evidenced first, sharply, over Empire.

Father started it.

"Of course," he remarked, with a sly sort of assurance, "of course, after the war, one of the preconditions of any lasting peace will have to be the greatest possible freedom of trade."

He paused. The P.M.'s head was lowered; he was watching Father steadily, from under one eyebrow.

"No artificial barriers," Father pursued. "As few favored economic agreements as possible. Opportunities for expansion. Markets open for healthy competition." His eye wandered innocently around the room.

Churchill shifted in his armchair. "The British Empire trade agreements," he began heavily, "are—"

Father broke in. "Yes. Those Empire trade agreements are a case in point. It's because of them that the people of India and Africa, of all the colonial Near East and Far East, are still as backward as they are."

Churchill's neck reddened and he crouched forward. "Mr. President, England does not propose for a moment to lose its favored position among the British Dominions. The trade that has made England great shall continue, and under conditions prescribed by England's ministers."

"You see," said Father slowly, "it is along in here somewhere that there is likely to be some disagreement between you, Winston, and me.

"I am firmly of the belief that if we are to arrive at a stable peace it must involve the development of backward countries. Backward peoples. How can this be done? It can't be done, obviously, by eighteenth-century methods. Now—"

"Who's talking eighteenth-century methods?"

"Whichever of your ministers recommends a policy which takes wealth in raw materials out of a colonial country, but which returns nothing to the people of that country in consideration. *Twentieth*-century methods involve bringing industry to these colonies. *Twentieth*-century methods include increasing the wealth of a people by increasing their standard of living, by educating them, by bringing them sanitation—by making sure that they get a return for the raw wealth of their community."

Around the room, all of us were leaning forward attentively. Hopkins was grinning. Commander Thompson, Churchill's aide, was looking glum and alarmed. The P.M. himself was beginning to look apoplectic.

"You mentioned India," he growled.

"Yes. I can't believe that we can fight a war against fascist slavery, and at the same time not work to free people all over the world from a backward colonial policy."

"What about the Philippines?"

"I'm glad you mentioned them. They get their independence, you know, in 1946. And they've gotten modern sanitation, modern education; their rate of illiteracy has gone steadily down. . . ."

"There can be no tampering with the Empire's economic agreements."

"They're artificial. . . ."

"They're the foundation of our greatness."

"The peace," said Father firmly, "cannot include any continued despotism. The structure of the peace demands and will get equality of peoples. Equality of peoples involves the utmost freedom of competitive trade. Will anyone suggest that Germany's attempt to dominate trade in central Europe was not a major contributing factor to war?"

It was an argument that could have no resolution between these two men. The words went on, but the P.M. began again to get a tighter grip on the conversation. He no longer spoke sentences, he spoke paragraphs, and Commander Thompson's worried, glum look began to clear. The P.M. gathered confidence as his voice continued to fill the room, but there was a question unanswered here, and it would remain unanswered through the next conference these men would join in, and the next after that. India, Burma—these were reproaches. Father, having once mentioned them aloud, would keep reminding his British hearers of them, sticking his strong finger into sore consciences, prodding, needling. And it was not from perversity, either; it was from conviction. Churchill knew that; that was what worried him most.

Smoothly he changed the course of the conversation, smoothly he involved Harry Hopkins, my brother, me—anyone to keep the subject away from Father and his mention of the colonial question and his nagging insistence on the inequalities of the Empire's favored trade agreements.

It was after two in the morning when finally the British party said their good nights. I helped Father into his cabin, and sat down to smoke a last cigarette with him.

Father grunted. "A real old Tory, isn't he? A real old Tory, of the old school."

"I thought for a minute he was going to bust, Pop."

"Oh," he smiled, "I'll be able to work with him. Don't worry about that. We'll get along famously."

"So long as you keep off the subject of India."

"Mmm, I don't know. I think we'll even talk some more about India, before we're through. *And* Burma. *And* Java. *And* Indo-China. *And* Indonesia. *And* all the African colonies. *And* Egypt and Palestine. We'll talk about 'em all. Don't forget one thing. Winnie has one supreme mission in life, but only one. He's a perfect wartime prime minister. His one big job is to see that Britain survives this war."

"I must say he sure gives the impression he's going to do just that."

"Yes. But you notice the way he changes the subject away from anything postwar?"

"It's embarrassing, the things you were talking about. Embarrassing to him."

"There's another reason. It's because his mind is perfect for that of a war leader. But Winston Churchill lead England after the war? It'd never work."

As it turned out, the British people agreed with Pop on that one.

Around eleven the next morning, the P.M. came to the captain's cabin on the *Augusta* again. He was with Father for two hours, and his business was the Charter. He and Cadogan and Sumner Welles and Harry Hopkins and Father were huddled over the most recent draft until lunchtime. I was in and out of the cabin during those two hours, just hearing bits and ends of conversation and wondering all the time how Churchill was going to square the sentiments in the Charter with the things he'd been saying the night before. I guess he was wondering too.

It ought to be set down that Sumner Welles was the man who worked hardest on the Charter, and who contributed most. It was his baby, from the time it was first considered, back in Washington; he'd flown from Washington with a working draft of the final agreement in his briefcase; and all the world knows how important a statement it was and is. It certainly isn't his fault, nor Father's either, that it hasn't been better lived up to.

Anyway, they toiled away at word changes until around lunchtime, when the P.M. left with his aides to go back to his own ship. Father was busy during the early part of the afternoon, taking care of mail and bills from the Congress that needed his attention; the plane was to fly back to Washington that afternoon.

About the middle of that Monday afternoon, Churchill was able to grab a few minutes for relaxation. From the deck of the *Augusta,* some of us watched him start off from the *Prince of Wales,* bound for a walk and a climb of the bluff overhanging the beach. First a whaleboat was lowered and manned by British sailors, who rowed it about to the companionway. Then down the steps scuttled the P.M., clad in a one-piece jumper with short sleeves and trousers cut off above the knees. From where we stood, he looked like some outsize fat boy, lacking only a toy bucket and spade for his afternoon's romp on the beach. Once in the whaleboat, he made straight for the tiller, and took vocal command. We could hear his barked orders, as they floated across the water—the sailors all bending to their oars with a will. At length we lost sight of him and his party, but we heard what happened next. The P.M. plunged up the bluff, which rose three or four hundred feet above the beach. Once there, he peeked over the brink and noticed a number of his party stretched comfortably out on the sand, hoping for a few rays of sunlight. Promptly Mr. C. gathered up a handful of rocks, and amused himself by scattering his dismayed followers with a few well-aimed tosses. High jinks in high places!

That night at seven, the P.M. was back with us for

dinner. This time our evening was really informal: only Harry Hopkins, Franklin Junior, and I were with the two leaders. It was a time for relaxation; despite the argument of the evening before, we were one family, talking slowly and easily. Still on the Englishman's mind was his desire to convince us that the United States should declare war on Germany forthwith, but he knew that he was waging a losing battle in that regard. The reports of the conferences of our military opposites had been coming in steadily in the past days: the awareness was growing on both sides, if there had ever been real doubt, that England depended on American production and American action for the ultimate victory.

And any realization of this sort was bound to have its effect on the relationship between the two men. Gradually, very gradually, and very quietly, the mantle of leadership was slipping from British shoulders to American. We saw it when, late in the evening, there came one flash of the argument that had held us hushed the night before. In a sense, it was to be the valedictory of Churchill's outspoken Toryism, as far as Father was concerned. Churchill had got up to walk about the room. Talking, gesticulating, at length he paused in front of Father, was silent for a moment, looking at him, and then brandished a stubby forefinger under Father's nose.

"Mr. President," he cried, "I believe you are trying to do away with the British Empire. Every idea you entertain about the structure of the postwar world demonstrates it. But in spite of that"—and his forefinger waved —"in spite of that, we know that you constitute our only hope. And"—his voice sank dramatically—"*you* know that *we* know it. *You* know that *we* know that without America, the Empire won't stand."

Churchill admitted, in that moment, that he knew the peace could only be won according to precepts which the United States of America would lay down. And in saying what he did, he was acknowledging that British colonial policy would be a dead duck, and British attempts to dominate world trade would be a dead duck, and British ambitions to play off the U.S.S.R. against the U.S.A. would be a dead duck.

Or would have been, if Father had lived.

At lunch the next day, Britain's Minister of Supply, little Lord Beaverbrook, joined the conference. At the same time, the military "opposite numbers" were at work in Admiral King's cabin. By two-thirty, everybody had reached final agreement on the joint statements that were to be issued. The principal diplomatic job of the weekend had been completed, and I know Welles and Father were pleased and proud. As everybody crowded out onto the *Augusta's* quarterdeck, the general impression was of one great big smile; the honor guard and the ship's band formed ranks; as the British chiefs of staff preceded Churchill over our cruiser's side, the band played *God Save the King.* The work of the conference was over. Next day it would be announced by the President and the Prime Minister on behalf of the United States and the United Kingdom:

1. That their countries seek nc aggrandizement, territorial or other;

2. That they desire to see no territorial changes that

do not accord with the freely expressed wishes of the peoples concerned;

3. That they respect the right of all peoples to choose the form of government under which they will live; and that they wish to see sovereign rights and self-government restored to those who have been forcibly deprived of them;

4. That they will endeavor, with due respect for their existing obligations, to further the enjoyment of all States, great or small, victor or vanquished, of access, on equal terms, to the trade and to the raw materials of the world which are needed for their economic prosperity;

5. That they desire to bring about the fullest collaboration between all nations in the economic field with the object of securing, for all, improved labor standards, economic adjustment and social security;

6. That after the final destruction of the Nazi tyranny, they hope to see established a peace which will afford to all nations the means of dwelling in safety within their own boundaries, and which will afford assurance that all the men in all the lands may live out their lives in freedom from fear and want;

7. That such a peace should enable all men to traverse the high seas and oceans without hindrance;

8. That they believe that all of the nations of the world, for realistic as well as spiritual reasons, must come to the abandonment of the use of force. Since no future peace can be maintained if land, sea or air armaments continue to be employed by nations which threaten, or may threaten, aggression outside of their frontiers, they believe, pending the establishment of a wider and per-

manent system of general security, that the disarmament of such nations is essential. They will likewise aid and encourage all other practicable measures which will lighten for peace-loving peoples the crushing burden of armaments.

This statement seems to me to have a peculiar and bitter historical interest, especially in the light of the later violations of its spirit and letter.

Leaving the first two points aside, with perhaps a passing nod to the natives of the Bikini atoll, who were removed in order to make room for civilization to experiment with its most fascinating new toy, we come to the third point, and take time to reflect on the peoples of Java and Indonesia. Pass over the fourth point; its mysteries are too deep. The fifth constitutes today a pious echo of our once-high hopes. The sixth still waits, at this writing, on the morrow. The seventh seems safe, at the moment (although perhaps citizens of the twentieth century would as soon see it applied to the airlanes as well as to the sealanes). The three remarkable sentences of the last point are especially cogent today: they should be drummed into the ears of men like Major General Groves, whose insistence on an ever-growing stockpile of atom bombs seems increasingly to be taking the place of a mature and considered American foreign policy.

Just before five o'clock, Tuesday afternoon, the *Prince of Wales* got under way, headed back for the wars. She slipped by close to the *Augusta,* which gave her passing honors, while the band played *Auld Lang Syne.* I was at Father's side, his arm on mine, as the British warship stood out to sea. About all we had time to say to each other was a fast goodbye, for the *Augusta* herself was scheduled to sail shortly. The weather was thick; there was no chance of flying back to Gander Lake. Eventually, Lord Beaverbrook and I were set ashore, forced to take a train back up to my base, where I would get him a seat on a plane bound for Washington and further conferences with our Lend-Lease officials.

The "Beaver" and I made the trip back to Gander Lake on a train that was a real antique: wooden seats, a pot-bellied stove in the middle of each car, a twenty-minute wait at every tenth-mile stop. Our uncomfortable ride didn't sit well with my astonishing little companion. When an inoffensive trainman made an understandable error, and misdirected us, the Beaver let him have it for nearly three minutes in a wonderfully shrill voice, interlarding his choicer comments with some of the more pungent Anglo-Saxon four-letter words. That trainman must have been either a philosopher or deaf, to take such abuse without complaint.

Whenever I wasn't distracted by these pyrotechnics, I was trying to assay the significance of the last few days. The English had come to beg for aid, but proudly, almost defiantly. Our leaders, while conscious of the fact that the United Kingdom was locked in a battle which was on our behalf, on behalf of all Americans, nevertheless represented people who did not yet realize clearly and completely without confusion the dangers which confronted them. America was still in flux from peace to war. Our chiefs of staff had the delicate task of weighing British demands against Soviet demands, making sure that each of these warrior-nations received from us enough aid to keep them killing Nazis.

I was impressed with the record of those days then, and I still am today. American destiny was in firm hands, in the hands of men who had striven and were still striving desperately to keep our country at peace, no matter what the means, while still protecting the longest-range national interests.

Time was still an important element, in the gamble the President and his chiefs of staff made that August, in the harbor at Argentia. As we know today, the time was running out, at a rate almost too fast for our production quotas to keep pace with it.

3

FROM ARGENTIA TO CASABLANCA

The relative inaction of reconnaissance in the Arctic was doubly hard to bear after the talk of action I had listened to at Argentia. Fortunately, my squadron was ordered back to the States early in September, barely a fortnight after the conference broke up. I promptly put in an application to go to navigation school, so that I might get—if not a pilot's rating—at least a navigator's rating, and be that much closer to overseas assignment. Mentally I underlined the application and added exclamation points, and maybe it did some good. For toward the end of September, my application was accepted, and I got orders assigning me to Kelly Field, at San Antonio, Texas. I had been a ground officer, an intelligence officer, now I would be an air officer.

In my notes covering those first days back in the States, those first days at Kelly Field, I find references on nearly every page to the air of complacency on every hand. It was bound to strike me, who had come from duty outside the country; I'm sure it struck everybody back from a visit to England, during this time; in a way, it shouldn't have surprised me so much. But when friends would tell me (as three different friends actually did) that it was high time I got out of uniform, that I'd spent my year in the Army, that I was losing out on some rich opportunities to cash in on the improved business conditions—my reaction was first to argue, later to wonder where this leathery insensitivity to what was going on in the world came from, and finally just to clam up and keep quiet about it. There was little use arguing the point, in September and October of 1941. I had an idea where the complacency came from, too, an idea which will surprise nobody by its novelty. The complacency was fed by a most important section of the American press. The Chicago *Tribune*, the Hearst papers, the New York *Daily News*, the Washington *Times-Herald*, and the Scripps-Howard papers: sometimes in unison, sometimes in harmony, they sang a sweet siren's song of indifference, placidity, passivity. If this dulcet chorus reflected the national temper of the people, then the newspapers had vacated their responsibility of bringing light and information. If the publishers thought they were shouldering this responsibility, then their conception of light and information must be given a very unpleasant name.

The first weekend in December, I had a pass to visit my family, at my ranch outside Fort Worth. I was scheduled to be graduated from navigation school in a few days (if all went well); I didn't know, of course, where I was going to be assigned, so I wanted to spend a day or two at home, visiting with my children.

Sunday morning I slept late, and just as soon as I'd had

some breakfast, I went horseback riding. I was back at the ranch about three that afternoon; Harry Hutchinson and Gene Cagle had called from my radio station on the telephone, my wife said. I figured they were just trying to make sure they'd have a chance to talk over business details before I drove back to San Antonio. And I didn't want to talk business. One of the children turned on the radio, to get some music, and then I knew why Harry and Gene had called. The radio hadn't been going long before I heard one of the broadcast orders that all officers and men should report back to their stations. Immediately.

While all of us talked at once, I changed out of my ranch clothes, and back into my uniform, called the adjutant at Kelly Field, and was told I'd better get back to camp by car that afternoon. There was no time except for the wildest speculation, and for questions from the children: What was Pearl Harbor? Where was it? The sedan was sent around front, and I hurried my goodbyes, and started south.

On the road to San Antonio, I passed hundreds of other service men hitch-hiking rides to their stations. There was room for four in my car: I drew one from Massachusetts, one from East Texas, one from West Texas, and a soft-drawling youngster from North Carolina.

At Kelly, everybody was as excited and confused as I was, and the rumors were getting bigger with every passing hour. After I'd checked in and reported to the adjutant and the officer of the day, I went back to the apartment I'd rented near the field, and put through a call to

Father. It took two hours for the call to go through, and I was in a thicker lather with every minute of those two hours that went by. At length the phone rang, and I picked it up. On the other end was Miss Hackmeister, the chief operator on the White House switchboard.

"Hello?"

"Captain Elliott?"

"Hello, Hacky . . . Father busy?"

"I'll put you right through. Just wanted to make sure it was you."

There was a moment's pause, and then I heard Father's voice.

"Elliott?"

"Hello, Pop!" I was nearly shouting.

"How are you, son?"

"Me? *I'm* fine. How are *you*?"

"Well . . . pretty busy, of course. . . ."

"What's the dope, Pop?"

"The dope? Well . . . of course, things look pretty serious. . . . What's news with you?"

"With me?"

"Yes. What do you hear?"

"Well . . . there's a story that we're all going to be shipped out tomorrow. . . . All squadrons to be ordered out to the Philippines. . . ."

"Really?"

"Then we heard not long ago that there was a Jap landing force in Mexico. And that there'd be an air attack on the Texas air bases any time now."

"I see."

"Then there was a story going around that the Japs

were getting ready a task force of ground troops—infantry—to come up from Mexico across the border and attack either Texas or California. . . ."

I could hear him grunt an interested affirmative. "Well," I heard him say, "if you hear anything else, you'll let me know, won't you?"

"Sure, sure, Pop! As soon as I . . ."

I could hear his phone click, as he set it back in its cradle. I hung up, too, and started . . .

Hey!

What was going on here, anyway? I call him up to find out the news, and all that happens is that *I* tell *him* . . .

And he wanted me to let *him* know if *I* heard anything else new. The Commander-in-Chief and the captain.

I sighed and went to bed.

Pearl Harbor or no, my navigation class continued its sessions according to schedule, until the appointed day for graduation. My orders sent me to the Sixth Reconnaissance Squadron, then located on the West Coast, with headquarters at Muroc Dry Lake, in the desert near Lancaster, California. Our job was patrol work over the Pacific. Until late in January, I served first with the Sixth and then with the Second; then, unexpectedly, secret orders came through directing that I report to the commander of the First Mapping Group at Bolling Field, in Washington.

There was so much secrecy attending my orders, and the nature of my future assignment, that my hopes were really soaring. *Must* be something big and important. Surely some sort of overseas assignment. . . .

Well, it was an overseas assignment, all right, but when I found out what it was, I was a little disgusted. It had a code name: RUSTY PROJECT, and it seemed so tame to me it was more than rusty, it was broken. I was one of two navigators to be assigned to do aerial intelligence and mapping photography of large parts of northern Africa. Africa!

Just before we left, I had a talk with Father, one of our after-breakfast-before-the-day's-work chats, during which I told him with some disappointment about my supposedly "super" assignment. To be sure, it was top-secret, but I figured it was possible the Commander-in-Chief knew about it already.

He did, and he quickly undertook to explain to me why my job was in fact more important than I had theretofore believed. Like all of his explanations, it also served to give me more perspective on the problems and strategies of global warfare, too. He began by glowing with pleasure when I told him what my job was to be. While I was grousing about it, telling him why I didn't think it was worth all the shouting, he was making himself another pot of coffee (Pop always made his own coffee; claimed they didn't know how to brew proper coffee down in the kitchen).

At length, when I was through beefing about what I thought was the unimportance of my job:

"You're wrong," he said. "You think you're being sent over just to take pictures of a lot of desert sand, and that it's a waste of time and film. But it isn't. Look at it this way. Is it important to keep China in the war?"

"Sure . . . I suppose so."

"Without China, if China goes under, how many divisions of Japanese troops do you think will be freed—to do what? Take Australia, take India—and it's as ripe as a plum for the picking. Move straight on to the Middle East. . . ."

"Japan?" I asked, incredulous.

"What's wrong with a giant pincer movement by the Japanese and the Nazis, meeting somewhere in the Near East, cutting the Russians off completely, slicing off Egypt, slashing all communications lines through the Mediterranean?"

"Well . . . but where does Africa come in?"

"At the moment, how do we get aid to China? Military supplies?"

"The Burma Road."

"And if it falls?"

"Fly it in from India?"

"That's it. That'll be the only quick way. Now: to get the matériel to India . . ."

"I see. The Mediterranean."

"Take it from another angle. You know how tough it is to guarantee shipments to the Soviet Union. The Murmansk run . . ."

"Murder."

"So now we're planning on the Persian Gulf. Will we have to continue thinking in terms of shipping supplies all the way around the southern tip of Africa? And don't forget, even on the island of Madagascar, there are men who wouldn't think twice of sheltering Japanese or Nazi submarines. We need the Mediterranean route. So . . ."

"Africa. I get it. The thing that kept me from getting

it before is—why we're spending time this way. Why we're not just loading up and socking the Nazis ourselves —from England."

"Don't we wish now that we'd been able to get production going full-steam faster." Father smiled a wry smile. "Don't we wish a lot of things. What we *know* is this: the Chinese are killing Japanese, and the Russians are killing Germans. We've got to keep them doing just that, until *our* armies and navies are ready to help. So we've got to start sending them a hundred—a thousand—times as much matériel as they've gotten from us so far. Africa is our insurance they'll get it.

"Look at Africa from another angle. The Nazis aren't in the Sahara just to get a sunburn. Why do they want Egypt? Why do they want central Africa? It's not a long hop from there to Brazil. Pennsylvania Avenue can have its name changed to the Adolf Hitler Strasse, and don't think it can't!

"You take good pictures of that sand, and don't think for a second that it's just so much film!"

Steve Early poked his head in the door, and looked meaningfully and exaggeratedly at his watch. Father laughed.

"Two minutes, Steve," he said. The door closed. I guess I was looking kind of swamped, for Father lifted his eyebrows inquiringly at me.

"It's just that it's such a big job," I said. "And we're such a long way from being anything like properly prepared."

"Just figure it's a football game," Father answered. "Say we're the reserves, sitting on the bench. At the moment, the Russians are the first team, together with the Chinese, and, to a lesser extent, the British. We're slated to be the . . . what's the slang for the climax runner? The speed boy?"

"I know what you mean."

"Before the game is so far advanced that our blockers are tired, we've got to be able to get in there for the touchdown. We'll be fresh. If our timing is right, our blockers still won't be too tired. And . . ." He paused.

"Yes?"

"I think our timing will be right. First place, in spite of the handful of vocal defeatists in this country, the American people as a whole have the guts and the stamina to carry through the job.

"In the second place, God didn't intend this world to be governed by the few. He will give our allies and ourselves the strength to hang on and win."

The door opened. "Two minutes," said Steve Early. "Good luck," said Father. And I left.

Rusty Project for me meant Accra, on the Gold Coast, and Bathurst, in British Gambia, and Kano, in British Equatorial Africa, and Fort Lamy, in French Equatorial Africa (always Free French). It meant several months of painstaking work, mapping the whole of northwestern Africa from the air, by photographs, occasionally running into Fascist patrol planes, occasionally under fire, but by and large just getting a hot, dry job over with as expeditiously as possible. Months later, I got back to the States, only for July and August, and at that I had to spend most of my time back home in a hospital, throwing off amoebic dysentery and malaria. As soon as I was on my feet and declared fit by Army doctors, I was handed orders sending me to England as commander of the Third Photographic Reconnaissance Group. (While still in Africa, I'd gotten my majority; my new assignment involved a lieutenant colonelcy.)

I hadn't too much opportunity for talks with Father during my two months back in the States. Quite aside from the fact that most of that time I was in the hospital, he was overloaded with the grueling schedule of work. I managed to look in on him three or four times, never for more than a few minutes, and each time I was struck with the picture of fatigue and sense of controlled strain. These days were in many ways the blackest of the war for the Allies; Britain, China, and the Soviet Union were alike calling for more and more supplies; none was completely satisfied. Mistakes were being made, in those days, by men on every level of command and every level of leadership, the mistakes of individuals learning to do war jobs who had never done war jobs before and certainly were anxious never to have to do them again. The accumulation of these giant cares and concerns was showing through gray, in Father's cheeks, and my instinct was to talk of anything but the war, on the occasions when I saw him.

In England, my outfit was stationed at Steeple Morden, not far from Cambridge. Somewhere, on higher levels, the argument between British and American strategists that was to result in no attack launched on the

Channel coast *that* year was being won by the advocates of waiting until our advantage both in manpower and matériel was overwhelming; my group's work was photographic reconnaissance of Normandy and Brittany, but only as training and experience for Africa. I got down to Chequers, Churchill's country home, for one weekend toward the end of September, and took care this time to be slightly better prepared than on my last visit. After dinner he casually mentioned that he planned to talk to Father on the transatlantic phone that night, and would I care to say hello? I'm sure his studied nonchalance was an act; I like to think that it was his thoughtfulness that led him to remember that this day was my birthday, and that to talk with Father that way was as pleasant a birthday present as I could have been given. For the record, it took the Prime Minister something over two hours to get a call put through to the President of the United States, and then the official censor warned all parties to watch their language, and then Father was wishing me a happy birthday. Before we were through talking, he had hinted guardedly that I might see some member of the family soon, and not to be astonished.

Next morning I had to leave to rejoin my outfit. I was summoned up to Churchill's room to say goodbye. He was stalking about the room, clad only in a cigar. Ho, I thought; here's something to tell my grandchildren about.

"Some member of my family" turned out to be Mother. I heard about her visit first when I got a call from our embassy in London, the day before she was to arrive. I came in to London and met her at Buckingham Palace where she had gone immediately upon her arrival.

She was pursued by bad weather most of the time she was in England. Even the night she and I dined at Buckingham Palace, with the King and Queen, she was uncomfortable from the cold that filled all the great barn-like rooms of that edifice. There were no complaints, for clearly this was British austerity, and the Royal Family was taking it like everyone else in England who had insufficient fuel. And I should hate to have to pay the heating bills for the palace even when fuel was plentiful.

At dinner that night, besides our very pleasant host and hostess, there was Field Marshal Smuts (next to whom I sat, and to whom I talked about photographing Africa, operating under the confused notion that so long as I stayed on Africa, it would be one of his subjects, conveniently forgetting that his part of Africa was hundreds of miles from my part), and there was also Lord Louis Mountbatten, contriving to look as handsome and dashing and glamorous as his reputation. After dinner, we adjourned to the cellar bomb shelter, where we were shown the Noel Coward film *In Which We Serve,* which had just been completed. Mountbatten, of course, was model and inspiration for this film's principal character; he distracted us only slightly by keeping up throughout the screening a running fire of comments upon the experiences which had served as basis for the film's plots.

That night I sat up with Mother until all hours, in her bedroom, our teeth chattering with cold. By this time I knew that the African invasion was about to be undertaken; she knew it too, she told me later. But that night we both talked all around it, speaking very guardedly, both of us being extremely careful not to betray to each other the secret we both knew. She had one piece of news for me, though: that Father was hankering harder than ever to come over himself, to meet with Churchill and, they both hoped, with Stalin as well. She was pretty tired from her flight over, but was happy to agree to come out and review my outfit.

The weather, the day she came out to Steeple Morden, was especially arranged by the British-type devil who is assigned to the hellish task of mixing up British weather. It was cold, windy, sullen, and wet. When it wasn't drizzling, it was pouring. Mother—in the hands of a committee of British guides—was an hour late, while my unhappy outfit stood about on the tarmac in front of the administration building. At length she arrived, everybody cheered up, she went down the line with me, shaking something like two thousand hands, chatting with as many of the men as she could. Then we hurried her inside and gave her tea (her guides asked for whisky, but we made them drink it out of teamugs, so that Mother shouldn't know).

Next day, all of us who were to be part of the African invasion got orders restricting us to our bases.

Ground echelons of my command started for embarkation points in late October.

Air echelons took off for staging areas on November 5th.

On the 9th, we hit Africa, and my group was at work

from a captured airfield the next day, having flown in and landed while the fighting was still going on.

For the next two months there was nothing but constant work, of the hardest kind I'd ever done, with so many problems of an immediate, day-to-day character that I hadn't the slightest opportunity to worry about any other phase of the war than that which had as its center the Maison Blanche airdrome, just outside Algiers.

Then suddenly, on January 11, 1943, I got a call to report immediately to the Chief of Staff of the Allied Expeditionary Forces, Major General Walter Bedell Smith, at headquarters in Algiers. This time, thanks to the hint that Mother had dropped, I had a pretty good idea why "Beedle" wanted to see me.

But he didn't say. He just instructed me to fly Admiral Ingersoll down to Casablanca, and report on arrival to the field commander. The colonel in charge of the field at Casablanca confirmed my hopes. He had the time of his life, that colonel, in tipping me the secret. Your father, he said. Churchill, too. Stalin probably. And he told me I had to stay inside for a day and a half, until Father got there, to guard against the possibility that somebody might recognize me and guess that I was here to meet him.

4

CASABLANCA CONFERENCE

ABOUT THE TIME I was wiping the remains of my sixth non-powdered egg off my chin, Father and his party were in Brazil. I had still plenty of time to stretch, rest, forget the war for a time, say hello to any of my friends who might be around, and have a look at where I was.

And what had been done to it. Which was plenty.

This was the most southerly of the African rendezvous which we had hit on the night of Sunday, November 8th. My part of the operation had been over the shoulder of Northwest Africa, in Algeria; this was the first time I'd had a chance to see what Casablanca's attackers had been up against.

Now it was more than two months later, but still in the harbor below lay the French battleship *Jean Bart,* pretty mercilessly pounded. And the town itself, spreading upward from the harbor over the hillside, showed definite signs that war had passed this way. Now, in January, American troops and American jeeps and trucks crowded the rights-of-way; and above, among the pleasant villas and holiday homes of wealthy French colonials, the early African spring had touched everything with color. It was bright, it was warm, it was gay. It was the antithesis of Argentia, an eon ago.

I'm sure the meeting-place had not been set for Casablanca simply because that is Spanish for "White House." However it had happened to be selected, when it was, we dispatched Secret Service agents to the spot, under the command of Mike Reilly, to pick the actual site where the Very Important Persons would live and meet and talk. I ran into Mike that first afternoon I got there. He was grousing mildly about the complications that he'd had to face and solve when he had been given the assignment of making Casablanca as safe as the White House.

First off, there was the question of the small army of enemy agents and informers throughout the entire area of French Morocco. It had been only very recently that the Nazis had been driven out; the French fascists they'd left behind, with German money in their pockets, were in many cases still to be unmasked and arrested by our security forces. Nor were we any too far from Spanish Morocco, at Casablanca, and nobody was under any illusions as to the friendliness of Franco and the Falangists, in January of 1943.

As if all this wasn't trouble enough, only three weeks earlier the Nazis had staged a full-dress air-raid on Casablanca itself. It was probably only a shot in the dark; probably they'd been aiming at Patton's extensive gasoline dumps; actually, their bombs had all been spilled on non-military objectives, succeeding only in making enemies of the Arabs whose families had been killed. But that raid was enough and plenty to give Mike Reilly pause. A lot of extra anti-aircraft batteries were set up in and around Casablanca, and the Krauts started to speculate, on their short-wave service to North Africa. (In Berlin, Goebbels' small fry got close enough to the truth to report that General Marshall was on hand to confer with the British Chiefs of Staff.)

Headquarters for most of the officers of the Combined Chiefs of Staff who would be attending the conference was the Anfa Hotel, a pleasant resort hotel, unpretentious but very modern, small and very comfortable. A compound had been staked off, and barbed wire flung around the area surrounding the hotel; it was called Anfa Camp, and it included the villas that Father and Churchill would occupy. Beyond the barbed wire patrolled General Patton's troops, demanding credentials of all who entered or left the compound, and themselves wondering what was about to go on inside.

Inside the compound, while Father's big flying boat was somewhere over the South Atlantic between Brazil and British Gambia, I was nosing around, determining how good the mess would be, for the dignitaries about to arrive. C-rations for two months, and British rations for two months before that, had left my taste-buds and gastric juices in an uncritical condition; I was prepared to report that the mess officers had outdone themselves.

Tuesday, late in the afternoon, Mike Reilly and I went down to Medouina airport to greet Father and his party.

They were due a few minutes after six. We were standing just beside the parking area which had been assigned to Father's plane.

"Say!" A sudden thought had come to me. Mike Reilly grunted and looked at me. "I just happened to think. This'll be the first time Father's been in a plane since the summer of 1932, when he flew to Chicago to accept the nomination."

"It's a lot more firsts than that," Mike answered, and he looked as though he was thinking of the grief those "firsts" had caused him. "It's the first time any President has ever used a plane to travel outside the States. In fact, it's the first time a President has ever used a plane, inside or outside the country, on official or unofficial business." And he looked at me expressively, and pantomimed the wiping of sweat off his brow.

Presently (and right on schedule; we automatically glanced at our wrist-watches; Major Otis Bryan was within sixty seconds of the estimated time of arrival) Father's C-54 came in sight, wheeled around, and settled grandly on the strip. And I ran over to say hello. Father, of course; Harry Hopkins, Admiral McIntire, Captain McCrea, Colonel Beasley—a dozen and more. And nearly a dozen Secret Service agents, too, counting those who'd come in the advance party.

Father was in high spirits, not a bit tired. He was full of his trip, the things he'd seen: all the way back to the compound, in the heavy old French limousine someone had requisitioned from somewhere, he talked of flying.

"Of course, this wasn't the first time. In June of 1932 . . ."

"What're you talking about, Pop? I was with you on that trip!"

"Oh. That's right. But there were some flights—you were just a baby—when I was with the Navy. In naval airplanes. Inspection trips. The kind of flying *you'll* never know."

"Thank God!"

"But this was important to me, Elliott. It's great to be able to see what so many of our fliers are doing, the sort of conditions aviation's going through these days, and developments of flying. Gives me a perspective. . . ."

He talked of the flight that day.

"Flew over Dakar. It's not the usual route, you know, usually they fly overland . . ."

"I know, Pop. I've flown the route three or four times."

"All right, all right. It's old stuff to you. But give a newcomer like me a chance." He frowned and smiled at me, all at once. "Saw the *Richelieu* in the harbor at Dakar. And remind me to tell you about what things are like in British Gambia. Bathurst. Don't tell me: I know: you've been there. But I'll bet I found out more in one afternoon in Bathurst than you were able to find out in two months!"

He had, too.

Inside the compound, we drove straight to Father's villa, Dar-es-Saada. It was quite a place. The living room must have been twenty-eight feet high: it was two stories up, with great French windows that looked out on an extremely handsome garden. Presumably to protect the windows, the villa's owners had installed sliding steel curtains which could cover them completely; it couldn't have been better arranged, from Mike Reilly's standpoint. There was an improvised air-raid shelter outside, in the swimming pool next to the garden.

Three bedrooms inside. Two were upstairs, one for Harry Hopkins, the other for me and for Franklin Junior, who was expected in a day or so. The bedroom downstairs was Father's, and it warranted several adjectives, but "appropriate" is none of them. When Father got his first look, he whistled. "Now all we need is the madame of the house," he grinned. It was the bedroom of—fairly obviously—a very feminine French lady. Plenty of drapes, plenty of frills. And a bed that was—well, perhaps not all wool, but at least three yards wide. And his bathroom featured one of those sunken bathtubs, in black marble.

A few steps away was Mirador, Churchill's villa, and Harry Hopkins went over to bring him back to our place for dinner. That first night, besides Father, the P.M., and Harry, there were General Marshall, Admiral King, General Arnold—the Joint U. S. Chiefs of Staff and General Sir Alan Brooke, Admiral Sir Dudley Pound, Air Chief Marshal Sir Charles Portal—the British Chiefs. There was also Lord Louis Mountbatten and Averell Harriman.

People were tired, that first night, but it didn't stop anybody from enjoying himself. During dinner, the only collision of minds came over the secrecy—or rather the lack of it—surrounding this Casablanca conference. The officers present—especially the British officers, and Churchill sided with them—were worried about the possibility of a Nazi sneak raid, a hit-and-run affair, once they were sure there was something big going on. It was the British view that everybody should remove at once to Marrakesh. Father was "agin" it, and said so, often enough and forcefully enough to carry the day. Trouble was, he had to carry the day not only that Thursday, but Friday and Saturday and Sunday, too. Marrakesh kept cropping up in the conversation, no matter what we happened to be talking about.

After dinner, Father and Churchill sat down on a big, comfortable couch that had been set back to the big windows. The steel shutters were closed. The rest of us pulled up chairs in a semicircle in front of the two on the couch. Politics was to be the subject. During the next two or three hours, one after another of the generals and admirals would take his leave, until by midnight only Father, Churchill, Hopkins, Harriman, and I were left. The talk was a little circuitous. It concerned, broadly, two things: Stalin, and the tangled French political scene (Darlan was in his grave less than three weeks when this talk took place).

On the first subject, the first question was: Would Stalin be here? And the answer was no. He had refused, Father said, on two grounds: first, that he was directly concerned with military guidance of the Red Army (and every one of us was excited over the great news that was coming from the eastern front), and second, that we all of us knew what he would say if he did come to such a conference: Western front.

"In any event," said Churchill, "we can proceed without him. We'll be in constant communication. Whatever is planned, we can submit for his approval. Harriman is here."

And for his part, Harriman (then, of course, our Lend-Lease Administrator) reported that, aside from an all-out attack on Europe, what would be of most use for the Soviets was Lend-Lease shipments, and on time. Father was worried about our production schedules. They were not at the levels that had been promised, and this was bound to affect not only the eastern front, but our commitments to the British and our commitments to our own Army and Navy as well.

Nobody seemed to be much in the mood to plunge into business, that first night. There was a disposition to sit back, to yawn and stretch, to have a drink and relax. For Father, it was the first day away from the pressure of the war in many months, and the others had similar records. I busied myself filling glasses. Father and Harry began to question the P.M. about de Gaulle; the conversation switched to the second principal subject.

"De Gaulle," Churchill sighed, and lifted his expressive eyebrows.

"You've got to get your problem child down here," said Father. It was his nickname; from then on, throughout the conference, de Gaulle was the P.M.'s "problem child"; Giraud was the President's.

Nobody, to put it mildly, was any too happy over the political snarl precipitated by our invasion of North Africa. Any restatement here of that complicated venture would require mention of the fact that our political maneuverings saved American lives—and that was a military as well as a patriotic consideration of top importance. On the other hand, there can be no question now (as, in fact, there was no question in Father's mind then) that somebody had erred, and erred seriously. Two things seemed to be, on this first night, governing Father's approach to the question: first, he was anxious to arrive at the best and swiftest possible solution to what was becoming an intolerable mess; second, he realized that his State Department was committed to a course, and that for reasons of future diplomatic give-and-take it was important to save the State Department's face as completely as possible. When a mistake is made, it is not good; but it is no better to proceed as though no mistake has been made: this truism led him to his first approach. When a mistake is made by your subordinates, who will be every day for the coming years engaged in delicate negotiations with your allies who are nevertheless your competitors, it is not good either; but it will help nobody but your competitors if you leave your subordinates in the lurch: this truism led Father to his second—and contradictory—approach.

And in any event, on this first night it was obvious that Father was quite simply interested in listening to what Churchill had to say, and thus in attempting to arrive at what he was actually thinking.

"De Gaulle is on his high horse," the P.M. said. "Refuses to come down here. Refuses point-blank." He seemed to be enjoying his description of his own difficulties, for some reason. "I can't move him from London," Churchill would say, cheerfully. "He's furious over the methods used to get control in Morocco and Algeria and French West Africa. Jeanne d'Arc complex. And of course now that 'Ike' has set Giraud in charge, down here . . ." And he wagged his head sadly.

Gently at first, but firmly, and later with real insistence, Father demanded that de Gaulle had to be brought down, insisting that a provisional government could not be left to one man, whether it was de Gaulle or Giraud, that the good offices of both Frenchmen would be required to set up the structure which would govern France until she had been completely liberated.

I got the impression, during the evening, that Churchill and Anthony Eden must at some time in the desperate past have promised de Gaulle—tacitly if not contractually—that his would be the only say in the reconstitution of France. The P.M. was moving very cautiously throughout this conversation.

"*My* problem child," he said, "regards Giraud's official position down here as an unfriendly act to his Free French." His voice was solemn. Again I conceived the idea that he was not really concerned over the way his "problem child" was acting up. "He would like," Churchill went on, "to have sole judgment and sole discretion as to who shall be part of any provisional government. Of course, this won't do."

Father suggested that Britain and the United States must make strong representation to de Gaulle, make it clear to him that all support would be withdrawn immediately if he did not forthwith stop pouting and fly down to the conference. Churchill nodded. "I guess that would be best," he said. "But of course I can't answer at the moment for what he will do."

Well after midnight, the P.M. took his leave. Father was tired, but still in a talkative mood, excited after his trip, expansive, and happy to see me again. I sat with him while he got into bed, and afterwards kept him up for the time it takes to smoke two or three cigarettes. Not only was it fine to see him again, but there were some things that had come up during the evening that had perplexed me.

"Was I just imagining things," I began, "or isn't the P.M. really worried by de Gaulle's pouting?"

Father laughed. "I don't know. I hope to find out, in the next few days. But I have a strong sneaking suspicion"—and he accented those words—"that our friend de Gaulle hasn't come to Africa yet because our friend Winston hasn't chosen to bid him come yet. I am more than partially sure that de Gaulle will do just about anything, at this point, that the Prime Minister and the Foreign Office ask him to do."

"How come?"

"Interests coincide. The English mean to maintain their hold on their colonies. They mean to help the French maintain *their* hold on *their* colonies. Winnie is a great man for the status quo. He even *looks* like the status quo, doesn't he?"

This had overtones of the old argument I'd listened to, back at Argentia, only perhaps on a higher level. Father was grinning at some secret thought.

"What's it, Pop?"

"Thinking of Mountbatten," he answered. "You know why Winston has Mountbatten here with him? It's so that I can be filled up to the ears with arguments about how important it is to divert landing-craft to Southeast Asia."

I looked my astonishment and incredulity.

"Sure," he went on. "Burma. The British want to recapture Burma. It's the first time they've shown any real interest in the Pacific war, and why? For their colonial empire!"

"But what's that got to do with Mountbatten?"

"He's their choice for Supreme Allied Commander of a brand-new theater—Southeast Asia."

"But what about Europe?" I asked. "What about the cross-channel deal? And what about the 'soft underbelly of Europe'?"

"Don't worry. Mountbatten has a lot of charm, a lot of persuasion, but I doubt strongly he'll be able to show enough to convince Ernie King. Try taking some of our Pacific landing-craft away from *him!* Or try taking any of the Atlantic landing-craft away from *this* theater."

This Burma story worried me, even though Father sounded so confident that it wouldn't mean anything.

"It's all part of the British colonial question," Father was saying. "Burma—that affects India, and French Indo-China, and Indonesia—they're all interrelated. If one gets its freedom, the others will get ideas. That's why Winston is so anxious to keep de Gaulle in his corner. De Gaulle isn't any more interested in seeing a colonial empire disappear than Churchill is."

I asked Father where Giraud stood in all this.

"Giraud? I hear very fine things about him from our State Department people. Murphy . . ."

"Murphy?"

"Robert Murphy . . . who's been in charge of all our dealings with the French in North Africa, since before the invasion."

"Oh, yes . . . sure."

"He's sent back reports that indicate Giraud will be just the man to counterbalance de Gaulle."

"Counterbalance de Gaulle? I shouldn't have thought he needed counterbalancing. All the reports we get—you know, in the newspapers, and so on—tell of how popular he is, in and out of France."

"It's to the advantage of his backers to keep that idea alive."

"Churchill, you mean? And the English?"

Father nodded. "Elliott," he said, "de Gaulle is out to achieve one-man government in France. I can't imagine a man I would distrust more. His whole Free French movement is honeycombed with police spies—he has agents spying on his own people. To him, freedom of speech means freedom from criticism . . . of him. Why, if this is the case, should anybody trust completely the forces who back de Gaulle?"

And that took me back to what Father had said about Burma again. Of course, from Churchill's standpoint, there was logic in such an adventure. Recapture Singapore—a good, dramatic thrust; that would carry tremendous prestige for all the colonial peoples of Asia and the Near East. But the troops, the supplies, the landing-craft that would be needed for such an operation! The length of the supply lines! And besides, when these things were needed so importantly if we were to slug at Hitler!

Father yawned, and I started to get up, but he waved me back to my seat.

"Don't go yet," he said. "Night's still young. And besides, I want to talk."

He talked for a bit longer about de Gaulle, about how the British owned him body, soul, and britches, about how they had supplied him with all the money, matériel, and morale which he needed to establish the Free French government in London and to launch the underground operations in France. Again he seemed almost to be talking his thoughts out loud, rehearsing them, sorting them, getting them organized in his mind for the talks that were to begin the next day and continue for ten days more.

His thoughts turned to the problem of the colonies and the colonial markets, the problem which he felt was at the core of all chances for future peace. "The thing is," he remarked thoughtfully, replacing a smoked cigarette in his holder with a fresh one, "the colonial system means war. Exploit the resources of an India, a Burma, a Java; take all the wealth out of those countries, but never put anything back into them, things like education, decent standards of living, minimum health requirements—all you're doing is storing up the kind of trouble that leads to war. All you're doing is negating the value of any kind of organizational structure for peace before it begins.

"The look that Churchill gets on his face when you mention India!

"India should be made a commonwealth at once. After a certain number of years—five perhaps, or ten—

she should be able to choose whether she wants to remain in the Empire or have complete independence.

"As a commonwealth, she would be entitled to a modern form of government, an adequate health and educational standard. But how can she have these things, when Britain is taking all the wealth of her national resources away from her, every year? Every year the Indian people have one thing to look forward to, like death and taxes. Sure as shooting, they have a famine. The season of the famine, they call it."

He paused for a moment, thinking.

"I must tell Churchill what I found out about his British Gambia today," he said, with a note of determination.

"At Bathurst?" I prompted.

"This morning," he said, and now there was real feeling in his voice, "at about eight-thirty, we drove through Bathurst to the airfield. The natives were just getting to work. In rags . . . glum-looking. . . . They told us the natives would look happier around noontime, when the sun should have burned off the dew and the chill. I was told the prevailing wages for these men was one and nine. One shilling, ninepence. Less than fifty cents."

"An hour?" I asked, foolishly.

"A *day!* Fifty cents a *day!* Besides which, they're given a half-cup of rice." He shifted uneasily in his big bed. "Dirt. Disease. Very high mortality rate. I asked. Life expectancy—you'd never guess what it is. Twenty-six years. Those people are treated worse than the livestock. Their cattle live longer!"

He was silent for a moment.

"Churchill may have thought I wasn't serious, last time. He'll find out, this time." He looked at me thoughtfully for a moment. "How is it, where you are? How is it in Algeria?" he asked.

I told him it was the same story. Rich country, rich resources, natives desperately poor, a few white colonials that lived very well, a few native princes that lived very well, otherwise poverty, disease, ignorance. He nodded.

And then he went on to tell of what he thought should be done: France to be restored as a world power, then to be entrusted with her former colonies, as a trustee. As trustee, she was to report each year on the progress of her stewardship, how the literacy rate was improving, how the death rate declining, how disease being stamped out, how . . .

"Wait a minute," I interrupted. "Who's she going to report all this to?"

"The organization of the United Nations, when it's been set up," answered Father. It was the first time I'd ever heard of this plan. "How else?" asked Father. "The Big Four—ourselves, Britain, China, the Soviet Union—we'll be responsible for the peace of the world, after . . ."

"If," I interjected. "If." I was joking, but part serious-superstitious, too.

"When," said Father, firmly. "*When* we've won the war, the four great powers will be responsible for the peace. It's already high time for us to be thinking of the future, building for it. France, for example. France will have to take its rightful place in that organization. These great powers will have to assume the task of bringing education, raising the standards of living, improving the health conditions—of all the backward, depressed colonial areas of the world.

"And when they've had a chance to reach maturity, they must have the opportunity extended them of independence. After the United Nations as a whole have decided that they are prepared for it.

"If this isn't done, we might as well agree that we're in for another war."

Too late, I thought, for such a depressing thought.

"Three-thirty, Pop."

"Yes. Now I *am* tired. Get some sleep yourself, Elliott."

Friday, January 15

I came down to breakfast next day to discover that I'd already soldiered on some of my duties. It was ten o'clock, but a half-dozen of the people I was supposed to usher in, greet, and prime Father for, were hard at work with him in his bedroom. I looked in on them after I'd gulped down coffee: they were Marshall, King, and Arnold, Hopkins and Harriman; and now General Deane, secretary to the American Joint Chiefs of Staff, had joined them too. I listened long enough to find out that they were discussing the question of agenda at the meetings of the Combined Chiefs, not only for that day but for the next few days as well. There must be something tricky about agendas; it always surprises me that there are so many hours spent in figuring out what you're going to spend so many more hours talking about. In this case, they were at it until well after noon.

It was a magnificent day. Outside, in the garden, one glance at the oleanders and bougainvillea was all you needed to realize that we should have lunch out-of-doors. We were six: Hopkins and Harriman; Churchill and his aide, Commander Thompson; and Father and I. The talk was of the afternoon, and what it was to bring: Ike Eisenhower; Robert Murphy, who had finagled the Darlan deal; and so on. The P.M. also requested the opportunity to present General Sir Harold R. L. G. Alexander, commander of the Middle East Forces, in the event he should arrive. We ate pleasantly; we chatted; no one dwelt on any of the problems that were to present themselves.

Up to this point, our North African push had gone well, but not magnificently. We were getting ready to trap all Rommel's forces against the sea, but the military aspects of the operation were still a question mark. The afternoon, it was agreed, would give the needed picture of future military operations which would help in determining where we should strike next. Still an open issue was the cross-channel invasion at that time referred to as ROUNDUP, the second front in 1943. As always, during all our conversations, the Americans were forcing the issue, the British holding back.

After lunch, Churchill and his aide left, together with Harriman, and shortly thereafter, General Eisenhower arrived. He'd been sick, I knew from the one or two opportunities I'd had to see him recently; but he looked on the mend that afternoon. He'd had lunch with Marshall and King, and he plunged right into a progress report on the war in Africa. Father listened interestedly as General Eisenhower told of the difficulties with supplies over the single-track (and hardly modern) railroad along the north coast. Nor were the roads much help.

"Any difficulties with Nazi agents? Anything to fear from Spanish Morocco?" Father inquired.

"We're keeping our eyes on 'em, sir. They haven't tried anything yet, and I'm inclined to think they won't in the future."

"Got enough political problems on your hands as it is, I imagine," Father smiled. The General grinned an answer. He didn't say it, but he might well have: "Oh, my aching back!" He went on to tell of the character of the opposition our troops were facing in the Gafsa and Tebessa sectors; in those days the opposition was tough, while we were just beginning to learn about war first-hand.

"No excuses, I take it," said Father, at length.

"No, sir. Just hard work."

"Well? What about it? What's your guess?"

"Sir?"

"How long'll it take to finish the job?"

"Can I have one 'if,' sir?"

Father chuckled.

"With any kind of break in the weather, sir, we'll have 'em all either in the bag or in the sea by late spring."

"What's late spring mean? June?"

"Maybe as early as the middle of May. June at the latest."

It sounded lickety-split to me. Father looked satisfied, too.

Suave, smooth Robert Murphy came in for a few

minutes around five o'clock. He and the General and Father had only one subject: French politics. Murphy was anxious to fill Father in on Giraud, how competent he would be as an administrator, how ideal a choice he was for the Americans to back. I listened to this conversation for a few moments, and then, getting a permitting nod from Father, I slipped outside. The Combined Chiefs of Staff were scheduled to deliver to the P.M. and Father a progress report of what they'd accomplished during their sessions from lunchtime on, so I ducked around to the front door to greet them on their arrival. Churchill had shown up a few minutes ahead of time with three British officers in tow; he wanted Father to meet them before the 5:30 meeting started. He and I took them in. There were General Alexander, Air Chief Marshal Sir Arthur Tedder, and General Sir Hastings Ismay from the office of the Minister of Defense. Just as at Argentia, the British advisers seemed about to outnumber our staff officers two-to-one.

General Alexander had flown directly from his headquarters in the western desert*, where he was directing the pursuit of Rommel's Afrika Korps. He was probably Britain's most capable field officer, and that afternoon he presented a picture of a grim, tired, single-minded soldier. He was unshaven and wearing battledress, he was tanned and weary. He spoke shortly but illuminatingly about the work of the British hammer that was driving the Nazi back against our American anvil in central North Africa.

* "Western desert" means, of course, the desert in North*east* Africa. The only thing it's west of is Egypt; I guess that's enough for the British. They gave it the name.

At one point, when Father's attention was distracted for a moment, I leaned over to whisper in his ear.

"Pop: the idea is that there's an American opposite for each British officer for these staff conferences?"

"That's right."

"They've got Tedder. Why isn't Spaatz here?"

"Why, indeed? Slip out and catch Hap Arnold. Ask him to get Spaatz here as soon as he can come, if he can be spared."

"Tooey" Spaatz, who was my boss, flew in a day or so later, and sat in at subsequent staff conferences. Just to give you an idea, the Combined Chiefs of Staff meeting called to report to Churchill and Father that afternoon numbered nine British officers and only five American. But maybe our Chiefs talked twice as much. I wouldn't know. I wasn't present for that session.

After an hour and a half with the Combined Chiefs, Father had still another half-hour to go on business, for Averell Harriman looked in with Lord Leathers, Britain's Minister of Transport. It was one of those visits that was scheduled for "only five minutes," but it stretched thirty-five.

Finally, Father got a chance to drink the old-fashioned I'd made for him.

"I can use this," he murmured, and shifted comfortably on the couch.

"Things going okay?"

"I think so, I think so." He smiled at a memory.

"What?"

"Apparently the British mentioned Burma this afternoon." He sipped his drink complacently. "You know,

Elliott, we have a tough enough time convincing Admiral King that any shipping or landing-craft should be diverted to the Atlantic theaters—only the scene of the main war. Can you imagine how he felt when Burma was mentioned? He's a grand Navy man. 'Wars can only be won by sea power; therefore, the Navy's plans must be best; furthermore, only the Pacific theater is a naval theater; therefore, the Pacific theater must be the most important.'" He laughed. "That's not *exactly* his reasoning, but it's close enough, it'll serve."

"Pop," I interrupted.

"Hmmm?"

"Got a surprise for you. He came this afternoon."

And Franklin Junior walked in. We had a grand reunion. He'd been executive officer on a destroyer, the *Mayrant,* that had been in the action during the storming of Casablanca; he was anxious to tell us about it, and we were anxious to listen. We did, too, and so did General Marshall and General Eisenhower, who joined us a few minutes later for dinner. The talk of action, seeing action, being part of an invasion and the fight that follows—in which I was able to chime in a bit, too—got Father jealous, reminded him that he'd been up front in the last war, as Assistant Secretary of the Navy.

"And I'm going up front in this one, too."

Marshall and Eisenhower exchanged a look, and went on eating.

"Well?" pursued Father. "Why the silence?"

"Maybe silence is consent, Pa," put in my brother.

Marshall glared at him, and he buttoned a discreet lip.

"It's impossible, sir," said General Eisenhower.

"Out of the question," General Marshall agreed.

"Why? There can't be much danger. Did you two have any trouble, coming down here? How about it, Ike? Any attackers, at any point from Algiers to Casablanca?"

"We did the last couple of hundred miles in our parachutes, sir, with one engine out and another about to go. There wasn't anybody feeling very happy on that plane."

"But that's mechanical. The reason you don't want me to go up to the front is military. Is there any danger? There isn't, is there, Elliott?"

Now I was on the hook. Marshall and Eisenhower were both looking at me. I pantomimed that my mouth was full of food. "Can't talk," I murmured.

"Coward," said Father. He waited patiently, while I had to pretend to swallow. "Well?"

"It *is* fairly common, Pop, for transport planes to be attacked along the route from Oran and Algiers on to Tunisia. No kidding."

"How about a fighter escort?"

"Sir," Eisenhower pointed out, "a fighter escort around a C-54, especially after all the speculation over the Nazi radio . . . it would just draw attackers like flies to honey."

"Orders are orders, sir," said Marshall. "But if you give them, nobody in the U.S. Army from us on down will take responsibility." He was very serious, and Father was very disappointed, but was forced to agree. They compromised on a review of three divisions of Patton's troops north of Rabat, instead.

There was no business scheduled for the after-dinner hours. The two generals departed, after a time, and Franklin and I were left alone to chat with Father . . . of home, and the family, of Mother . . . the things any sons would say to their father during a brief leave. He'd brought over a bundle of New York and Washington newspapers, which we promptly dove into, discovering among other things that a Congressman named Lambertson had been complaining in the House of Representatives about the Roosevelt children, and the way they sat around boozing in New York night clubs while "American boys are fighting and dying far from home." At this time, my older brother Jimmy was with Carlson's Raiders, in action somewhere in the Pacific, and John was in training for sea duty as a supply officer. Well, well: there were also comic strips to read in those newspapers.

Father got to bed fairly early that night: before midnight. He needed the sleep.

Saturday, January 16

Next morning the P.M. was an early caller, for him. He arrived before ten and together he and Father spent the forenoon with Eisenhower, Murphy and Sir Harold MacMillan, the British Minister attached to Allied Headquarters. French politics again. Franklin and I—we hadn't seen each other since Argentia, in August of 1941; in fact, it was the first time I'd seen any of my brothers since then—stuck our heads in just long enough to discover that the substance of the talk was again de Gaulle and Giraud. By then, Churchill and Father had found an alternate for "your problem child" and "my problem child." Now it had been shortened to "D" and "G." Where was D? Why wasn't he on tap? Still the principal political concern was to thrash out if possible some viable solution for the French political snarl. I had seen enough of the newspaper stories from home, the night before, to realize what a first-rate diplomatic problem existed. It was the first time I had realized how much Murphy was on the pan. From what I overheard, at least some of the criticism seemed justified; his governing concern seemed to lead in the direction of ensuring that any future government in France include—on a dominant level—the same men that had been among the principal "appeasers" in the critical years before war broke out.

We had lunch out in the garden again: Father, Harry Hopkins, Franklin, and I were joined by George Durno, at that time a captain in the ATC. George had covered the White House for INS in the years before the war and was an old friend of Father's. Again it was a chance for Father to relax. The change was doing him good, despite the heavy schedule; he looked fit; some of the grayness was disappearing from his cheeks.

Over coffee, he got back on the theme of the development of colonial areas, increasingly one of his favorite topics. For a man who had never been in Africa before, he had picked up an amazing amount of information, geographical, geological, agricultural. Of course, I thought I knew the country pretty well: I had flown over a good bit of it, months before, photographing it from the air. But somewhere he had had a chance to learn even more than I had. We discussed the great salt flats in southern Tunisia, which must have at one time been a vast inland sea. He reminded us of the rivers that spring up in the Atlas Mountains, to the south, and disappear under the Sahara, to become subterranean rivers. "Divert this water flow for irrigation purposes? It'd make the Imperial Valley in California look like a cabbage patch!" And the salt flats: they were below the level of the Mediterranean; you could dig a canal straight back to re-create that lake—one hundred and fifty miles long, sixty miles wide. "The Sahara would bloom for hundreds of miles!" It is true. The Sahara is not just sand, it has an amazingly rich potential. Every time there is a rain, there is a consequent riot of flowers for a few days, before the dryness and the sun kill them off. Franklin and I winked at each other: Father was having the time of his life, his active mind and quick imagination working overtime as we all speculated on what intelligent planning could do for this land.

"Wealth!" he cried. "Imperialists don't realize what they can do, what they can create! They've robbed this continent of billions, and all because they were too shortsighted to understand that their billions were pennies, compared to the possibilities! Possibilities that *must* include a better life for the people who inhabit this land. . . ."

That afternoon, the American Joint Chiefs of Staff returned, again to bring Father up to date on plans thus far discussed with their British opposites. It developed that they were opposites in more ways than one, that the British chiefs had worked out with Churchill an agenda considerably differing from the American agenda reviewed by Father and Harry Hopkins, two mornings before. Instead of talk about massive thrusts against the flanks of Europe, the British were intent on smaller actions in the Mediterranean. This was the first time I heard Sicily mentioned, and there were other way-stations to victory mentioned, too: the Dodecanese Islands, for example, leading to Greece, and a push into the mountainous Balkans.

Sunday, January 17

Just at noon next day, the first callers arrived. They were General Charles Nogues, the Resident-General at Rabat, and General Patton and General Wilbur. Wilbur was on Patton's staff; he had come along, unnecessarily as it happened, to act as interpreter. Father's French was fluent and he chatted along with Nogues without help.

Nogues and Patton, for two generals who a scant few weeks ago had been fighting each other bitterly along the beaches of French Morocco, were surprisingly affable together. It was more than that they were both professional soldiers, who would not expect to carry their animosity beyond the battlefield. Actually, neither of them was political in more than the most casual sense. Each operated under orders, Patton—fortunately for us—far more efficiently than Nogues. Nogues had orders to resist, he resisted; subsequently orders came through to cease resistance, he ceased. New boss now.

As far as Father was concerned, this was primarily a courtesy call. There was another side to it, however; this man Nogues had been cited by the P.M. as one of the reasons for his difficulties in getting de Gaulle to come to Casablanca. Nogues—graduate of Saint-Cyr, the French military academy, professional soldier and colonial administrator, a man who wanted only to be given clear, understandable orders and subsequently left alone —was the center of a first-rate dispute. From London, as reported to us by Churchill, de Gaulle was insisting that his countryman and fellow officer Nogues be jailed forthwith as a collaborator; jailed and held for trial. Yet here in French Morocco, as we knew, General Patton (only very recently his enemy and bitter combatant) was insisting that Nogues be retained in his present position. Later, Patton was to file a vigorously partial report on behalf of Nogues; he was convinced that Nogues' influence with the Sultan of Morocco and with the native population could be very helpful to our military, so long as we used the country as a base.

On this warm Sunday afternoon, when Father put questions to the Frenchman about the people of Morocco, how their lot was to be improved, he looked blank. He had never troubled to figure out the answers to this question; it had never been put to him before. Yet he knew to the penny how much wealth could be exported from the country, to the sou how grievously the Moroccans could be exploited. The Sultan, Patton had given us to understand, was under Nogues' thumb, where he had been for years; Nogues wanted nothing except to keep him there. After Father had had an opportunity to meet and talk to this bone of de Gaulle's contention, and the generals had left:

"Make a note that the Sultan must come to dinner one

night, Elliott," said Father. "Find out from Murphy or whoever knows what the protocol involved is. This Nogues . . . he's not to be considered."

Nogues and Patton and Wilbur had left our villa for Churchill's; the P.M. stayed with them for some time, and then walked over to Dar-es-Saada to have lunch with us. He told us that that morning he had gone down to the harbor, to inspect the shelled hulk of the *Jean Bart*.

"You got to see the *Jean Bart*?" demanded Father, irritated. "By gosh, if you can get to see it, then I can."

We whooped with laughter. He was for an instant like a boy of six: *You* got some ice cream—*I* want some.

That afternoon General Mark Clark dropped in. Churchill had left, in his ears more of Father's admonitions about de Gaulle. Father was more and more confident with every passing day that Churchill was deliberately holding de Gaulle back, that he could produce his "problem child" at any time he cared. Now General Mark Clark was here, and he had news. For he had brought to Casablanca the American "problem child," Giraud. Now Father would have an opportunity to meet the man touted to him by Murphy and our State Department as the logical choice to back against the eventuality of one-man, British-backed control, as personified by de Gaulle. Father was alert and interested, anxious at last to meet the man entrusted with command of French armies in North Africa.

Clark stayed only long enough to make sure Father was ready to interview Giraud, then he was gone to fetch him. I think all of us in the villa were excited: the patient diplomatic maneuvering that had been occupying Father's mind vis-à-vis Churchill during the past days was about to resolve itself, we all hoped: here would be an important move in an important and difficult game. When Clark returned with Giraud, Murphy and Captain McCrea came too, and all settled down for the crucial talk.

It was a vast disappointment to Father.

As far as Giraud was concerned, there was no such thing as a political problem. There was only the military question of the war. Ramrod straight he sat his chair, never relaxing. Age alone had softened him, even his jail experiences had left no appreciable mark. As his early diffidence disappeared, a note of insistence crept into his tones.

"Only give us the arms," he cried. "Give us the guns and the tanks and the planes. It is all we need."

Father was friendly, but firm in his cross-examination. Where were his troops to come from?

"We can recruit colonial troops by the tens of thousands!"

And who would train them?

"There are plenty of officers under my command. It constitutes no problem. Only give us the arms. The rest . . ."

But the rest included problems he would never appreciate. Churchill had pointed out that tardiness in repealing the anti-Semitic laws originally promulgated under the former Vichy régime was one of the main causes of de Gaulle's pique—or at least one of the alleged causes. Giraud swept these questions aside. He was single-minded.

"The only thing that is needed is the equipment. A few weeks of training, and great armies will be available."

Father showed by his questions that he felt Giraud underestimated the job seriously. So intent was the French general on his own plans that I doubt whether he perceived Father's negative reaction. Giraud's conviction was tireless and limitless. But Father was giving away nothing.

And as soon as Giraud and the others were out of the room, Father showed by expression and gesture what he thought.

"I'm afraid we're leaning on a very slender reed," he said. He threw up his hands, and laughed shortly. "This is the man that Bob Murphy said the French would rally around! He's a dud as an administrator, he'll be a dud as a leader!"

Dinner that night, which involved the P.M., Lord Leathers, Admiral Cunningham, Admiral King, General Somervell, and Averell Harriman, had been arranged so that the important question of shipping priorities could be discussed and agreed upon. By this time the Combined Chiefs of Staff had combined to push the idea of any Burma operation out the window; the thinking was beginning to take form that the next Allied push would be against Sicily, to ensure the trade routes through the Mediterranean to the Persian Gulf, and on to the Soviet Union. But shipping was still scarce, still desperately needed; the Battle of the Atlantic, in that winter of 1942-43, was far from won. How many tons of shipping to be reserved for the job of stockpiling matériel in the

United Kingdom? How many tons to be diverted for shipment of arms to the Red Army? What percentage to be set aside for withdrawal of troops and supplies from the Mediterranean back to Britain? Could we depend on the African job being finished by May-June? How much to be allocated for Sicily? To British minds, subtractions could be made from the tonnage reserved for the Murmansk and Persian Gulf runs; to American minds, the biggest possible margin must be held for those vital jobs.

The conference on shipping went on until after one in the morning, and it went on without me. Franklin and I left Anfa Camp that night to join up with some younger officers at their mess.

Monday, January 18

Mark Clark and Murphy looked in on Father again the next morning, again to discuss the French political situation: they were together for about two hours, planning as carefully as possible the American policy on the setup of the interim French government, until that country could be liberated. In Father's mind our dilemma was at least now clearly defined: a serious overestimation of Giraud's qualities of leadership and an ambiguous policy of cooperation with Vichyite French colonials made very difficult American opposition to the one-man, British-backed government of Charles de Gaulle. The P.M. came to lunch, shortly after Murphy and Clark had left; our conversation at lunch was desultory, with Father and Harry Hopkins continuing to spar gently but pointedly with Churchill on the subject of de Gaulle's continued absence from Casablanca.

That afternoon Father had his first chance to leave the villa; he climbed aboard a jeep and, in company with General George Patton and Lt. Colonel C. E. Johnson, commanding officer of the Third Battalion of Patton's First Armored Corps, set off to inspect a guard mount of the infantry assigned to protect Anfa Camp. I was on hand to greet him when he returned.

"You should have seen the military band," he said. "There was a fellow must have weighed nearly three hundred pounds, playing on a flute that must have weighed all of four ounces!"

The Combined Chiefs of Staff were due at five o'clock, and they stayed for an hour and a half. Seven Britishers and four Americans had settled upon HUSKY, the invasion of Sicily. In a sense, we had been committed to the Sicilian deal once the decision to clear out North Africa had been taken. Now, by agreeing on HUSKY, a compromise had been struck between American inclinations toward the cross-channel invasion in the spring of 1943 and the British argument for capture of Sicily and the Dodecanese Islands, looking toward the invasion of Europe via Greece or the Balkans. Apparently Churchill had advised by-passing Italy and striking directly into what he termed "the soft underbelly of Europe." Always he was of the opinion that we should contrive our entry into Europe in such a way as to meet the Red Army in central Europe, so that Britain's sphere of influence might be maintained as far east as possible.

HUSKY was regarded as an important step forward in any event, by both Americans and British. And by committing the Allied armies to the invasion of Sicily and the hoped-for elimination of Italy from the war, we were recognizing that the cross-channel invasion would have to be postponed until the spring of 1944.

That afternoon, Father and Churchill agreed to notify Stalin of Anglo-American strategy. And that afternoon, the thoughts of the two statesmen were turned to the formulation of a joint statement on the war, to be addressed to the Axis enemy.

A quiet, unofficial dinner; afterwards Franklin and I went downtown. I had supposed that Father would be in bed and asleep early. In bed he was, but not asleep, when I got back to the villa around two in the morning. He was reading a twenty-five-cent reprint of the Kaufman-Hart play, *The Man Who Came to Dinner*, and chuckling over it; by his bedside lay *The New Yorker*, where he had tossed it when he finished it. He had stayed up because he wanted to hear all about our evening; as always, he was envious of our relative freedom, and listened to my story with the greatest gusto. In truth, the evening had been dull: a trip through the local *kasbah*, with a couple of Shore Patrolmen as our guides; but I did my best to liven it up with imagined details.

Tuesday, January 19

The next morning, I had my hands full with a sleepy brother. Franklin was due back aboard his destroyer, and he barely made it. Harriman and Murphy were at work with Father early, laying the groundwork for his second conference with Giraud. The French general arrived at noon, and he was still preoccupied solely with the military details of his vague future. Father undertook to outline U.S. foreign policy, as it regarded France during the war:

> The provisional government must be set up, and must be set up with Giraud and de Gaulle equally responsible for its composition and welfare;
>
> This provisional government must undertake to run France until the country's liberation was complete.

Giraud was unenthusiastic, but he had no counterproposals, he had no special area of disagreement, he was simply concerned with how completely U.S. arms would be accorded him for his colonial armies.

Harry Hopkins signaled to me, as this conversation was drawing to its unexciting close.

"Your father wants to buy some souvenirs, as presents when he gets home. Want to come along with me?"

"Sure."

"We'll probably have to wait until after lunch. And I think they want to have some pictures taken—your father and Giraud together."

So after lunch, General Patton called in his staff car, and with him Harry and I went downtown. Rugs and some rather poor quality Moroccan leather goods—that was all that was to be found. We arranged to have some of the rugs sent up to the villa, so that Father could have a look at them himself and make his own selection, and then we rode through the waterfront area for a time, having a look at the beaches and shoreline our troops had hit, some weeks before.

Back at Dar-es-Saada, we found that Churchill had dropped by, with his son, Randolph, at that time a captain in the Commandos. I had met Randolph once before, in Algiers on Christmas Eve. I had looked forward to talking with him, for I knew he was a Member of Parliament as well as a Commando officer. After such looking forward, such disappointment! I had discovered, that Christmas Eve in Algiers, that for young Randolph Churchill conversation is strictly a unilateral operation.

Now that I found young Mr. Churchill in Father's villa, I was really intrigued to discover whether his opinions would be as articulate with his father and mine as they had been with me. I rather think I had expected him to be somewhat daunted, but he held forth with remarkable loquacity and singular determination on every subject that he mentioned for the fifty minutes he was present. During that time he held the floor to explain all the intricacies of Balkan war-and-politics, to clarify for the statesmen present the shortest possible way in which they might preserve British hegemony in the Mediterranean while at the same time prolonging the world conflict by some years, to expose the faults in the plan of campaign as set forth by the Combined Chiefs of Staff for a Prime Minister and a President, and to set at ease the worries of the same Prime Minister and President on the ticklish question of French politics. It was a remarkable performance, and one that held his audience's interest—not so much from their five days' fatigue as from their amused detachment. (Perhaps I should except young Randolph's father from this inclusive paragraph, but I have set down accurately my own reaction, and that of my father, who was able to restrain his smiles only until young Randolph had taken his departure.)

After they had left, Father and I had a few minutes alone together, before once more General Patton's staff car was outside, waiting to take us to his headquarters, Villa Mas, for dinner. Around the dinner table that night there were Rear Admiral C. M. Cooke, Jr.; Major General Geoffrey Keys, Patton's Deputy; Brigadier General A. C. Wedemeyer; Brigadier General W. H. Wilbur; Brigadier General John E. Hull; and Colonel H. R. Gay. Most of these officers were commanders of the First Armored Corps, and all of them had apparently been awaiting an opportunity to bend the ear of a President of the United States on the subject of the unparalleled supremacy of tanks and armored units generally in modern warfare. In this chorus, Patton took the lead tenor, with the others decorously joining in and supplying harmony. Aircraft? Infantry?

"Armor!" Patton exploded. "Modern warfare has developed to the point where most if not all the fighting will be done by tanks and armored mobile vehicles. Infantry? What's it got to do, beyond mopping up, and securing the ground captured by the tanks?"

I imagine that it was I who put in a word about aircraft.

Patton was politely disparaging.

"Of course, it has its rôle. I would be the last to say that the air forces were worthless. There's no question in my mind but what airplanes can be helpful in supporting the armored ground operation. . . ."

Beyond that one oar, loyally stuck in on behalf of the air forces, I maintained a discreet silence. For his part, Father ate and relaxed and enjoyed himself. He was certainly not going to allow himself to get involved in any intra-military imbroglio. So General Patton held the floor at his will. (And a month or so later, when he took command of the southern front in Tunisia, I would be amused to recall this conversation, while listening to the two-way radio at our African headquarters pour out frantic requests from Patton's command for more air reconnaissance, more tactical air support—*in advance of his armor.*)

The General's Casablanca headquarters was a showplace. Prior to our conquest, his villa had been the center for the Nazi mission to French Morocco, and when the enemy had left, he had left so fast that he had not had time to strip it of any of its rich and magnificent furnishings. And General Patton was as pleased as a boy, showing us around among its splendors.

Father and I returned to our villa shortly after eleven. On the way back, he spent most of the time kidding me about armor versus air forces. He was feeling perky, and he showed it. Five minutes after we arrived, Churchill was with us, for a drink and a chat about de Gaulle and Giraud. The P.M. returned once more, obliquely, to his contention that France's provisional government might better be left solely in the hands of de Gaulle; he knew how dissatisfied Father was with Giraud's potentialities. But this evening Father was in no mood to argue his point with the P.M. further; he dismissed the subject almost peremptorily. Perhaps because he was tired, he was not too tactful in making it quite clear that he was not interested in exploring the problem further. So Harry Hopkins and I combined to keep the conversation in carefully innocuous channels. Around one in the morning, Churchill left, and Harry went upstairs to bed.

Father and I went to his bedroom. Father said, "Now Winston's really beginning to get worried, himself. You could see it tonight."

All that I had seen was that Churchill had obviously wanted to bring the subject up, Father as obviously had refused to discuss it. I had put it down to the fact that Father was tired. Apparently it was tactics, and apparently each knew what the other was doing.

"The next two or three days will tell the story," Father said, now quite cheerfully. "This is Tuesday? I'll take a small bet Winston tells us no later than Friday that he thinks he'll be able to get de Gaulle to come down after all."

We talked for a time about Patton—"a delightful man, really, isn't he, Elliott?" and about young Randolph

Churchill—"It must be wonderful," was Father's comment, "to have so few misgivings"; and about the rugs which Harry and I had seen that afternoon. Father was inclined to worry about the effect on Stalin and the Russians of the military decisions which our Combined Chiefs had come to. "If 'Uncle Joe' had only been able to get here himself—see for himself the difficulties we face in shipping, the problems of production . . ."

Father was tired that night. I left him after a very few minutes.

Wednesday, January 20

The problems of production and supply were the first on the agenda, next day. Somervell had an early breakfast date with Harry Hopkins; they were hard at it when I came down about eight-thirty. Harry, of course, was head of the Priorities Board at that time; if there was anyone who was intimately aware of the fact that American war production was still only a comparative trickle, it was he.

My boss, Major General Spaatz, arrived around ten o'clock. He had got to Casablanca the day before, and Father had expressed a desire to chat with him personally. "Tooey" Spaatz at that time was the commander of all American Air Forces in Africa, and in addition he had command of the Northwest Africa Air Forces, which was a combined Allied air operating headquarters. Father commented that it sounded complicated. Spaatz nodded.

"It is, sir," he said. "And it's not made any easier by

the fact of combined command. There's none better than Tedder"—Air Chief Marshal Tedder ranked Spaatz, and had titular command of all Allied Air Forces in Africa—"but despite the fact that we get along together famously, there's no getting around some of the difficulties."

"Like what, exactly?"

"Well, sir: in this theater we use predominantly American planes. And strategy and tactics are predominantly American too. The operations are American. But the top command is British."

I put in a word. "Actually, Pop, General Spaatz is running the air war, but under Tedder."

"I don't want to suggest, sir," Spaatz went on, "that we aren't working well together. We are. All that I'm describing, I guess, is the difficulty of any Allied, any *combined* control. Combination of control gets specially tough when what the Allies are controlling is the men and matériel of just one of those Allies."

Father nodded. Tooey went on, talking about some of the other problems of his command: at that time they consisted principally of getting enough replacement planes and building enough hard-surfaced airfields. With the kind of fields we found in Africa, if there was a good wet rain we had to cancel operations for hours or maybe days at a time.

It was important for Father to have talks of this kind, with ranking American officers. The politics of being allied with the British were such that, granted an over-all American theater commander (Eisenhower), the

British insisted, perhaps quite properly, on getting the command posts next below. So a Britisher (Cunningham) was in charge of naval operations and a Britisher (Tedder) was in charge of air operations. In the Mediterranean, there was greater justice to turning naval operations over to a British officer. But Spaatz was having his troubles trying to run the war in the air, while simultaneously taking orders from an RAF marshal, despite the fact that the individual involved was a very competent and very pleasant officer.

Robert Murphy, like a well-oiled jack-in-the-box, popped in again that morning, to talk to Father and Harry Hopkins. The job was still to be accomplished of convincing de Gaulle's backers, the British, that we really meant our insistent demand that any provisional government would have to include other than merely de Gaulle's forces. They were still talking by the time Churchill and his adviser, MacMillan, arrived for lunch; hastily, I had some extra places set at the table in the garden, and the discussion went on.

Wouldn't the best way to find out exactly what were de Gaulle's objections to the projected provisional government be to get him down here? And right away? What sort of concessions did the P.M. think *might* have to be made to de Gaulle in order to get him down here, prepared to thrash out the problem once and for all? Were the Americans *sure* that Giraud was necessary to the future picture? Were there, in fact, any but subjective conflicts in the way of arriving at a viable, decent political alliance between the two?

At length the P.M. pushed his chair back and got up to go see Giraud himself once more. I kept an eye on Father's face, but all it showed was friendly interest. If he still harbored suspicions as to whether Churchill was playing a completely frank rôle he never showed it.

Late that afternoon, the P.M. was again ushered into the living room of Father's villa, and he had brought Giraud with him. This time I stayed outside, chatting with the secret service agents and occasional visitors. Inside, for the *n*th time, Father and the P.M. were painstakingly going over with Giraud and his civilian aide, a M. Poniatowski, the questions that had been raised by de Gaulle, were calculating the niceties of what would never be more than a shaky alliance, were patching up in at least unilateral fashion the subjective grievances between these two highly subjective French military leaders. This was ground I had heard gone over again and again. Father and Churchill must have been as tired of it as I, but at least I didn't have to stick with it.

When the others had left, and I went back in to rejoin Father, what I was thinking of was that that night we were to dine over at Churchill's villa, and that maybe this same subject would be the only one under discussion. As soon as Father looked up from a pile of papers that had come in from Washington, though, he set my mind at rest.

"We've agreed there's to be no more talk about business tonight, Elliott."

And the dinner in the Prime Minister's villa was indeed very pleasant. Being a war prime minister, Winston Churchill insisted on bringing the war plans of Empire with him. His aides had fixed up for him a magnificent war-room, with maps of all scales of all theaters. He had a lot of fun showing them to us; if war were only a game, and not a very bloody, messy, tedious, dispiriting affair, I think those maps would have been the best way to play at the game. On each there were pins, to be pulled out and stuck in at different points. Perhaps the most fascinating was the quite large picture of the North Atlantic, with all information about every Nazi submarine pack reduced to sliding miniatures: so many lying quiet at L'Orient and Brest, so many more prowling westward, toward our convoys bound for the United Kingdom, so many more in pens along the Channel, so many more lurking in the sea lanes about the Azores, so many more lying off Iceland, or pointing north, toward the Murmansk run. Each day, Churchill watched while the most recent information about ship movements was registered on this great chart; there was a sense of mighty suspense about it: would this convoy get through undamaged? How many tons of vital matériel would explode, and scatter, and sink to the ocean floor from that convoy? Would British coastal patrol get a chance at a good bomb-run over this wolf-pack? That winter, of course, the Battle of the North Atlantic would reach its height; and the suspense that was engendered in the tiny pins and miniatures of that Admiralty map was a global suspense, with the answer to world history caught up in its resolution.

We were home comparatively early that night, and

Father went straight to bed, for he had a long and tiring day ahead of him.

Thursday, January 21

He was up, breakfasted, and gone before I got downstairs. Hopkins went with him, and Harriman, and Admiral McIntire, and Murphy; General Clark was their host. From Casablanca north to Rabat they drove, where the President inspected the Second Armored, the Third Infantry, and the Ninth Infantry. They made quite a caravan: first a motorcycle unit of MP's, a jeep, and a recon car, then Father's sedan, then the rest of his party, in Army cars, then two trucks of heavily armed troops, two more recon cars, and a second motorcycle detail bringing up the rear. Mike Reilly of Secret Service had even made sure there would be an escort of fighter planes overhead, for the trip northward along the coastline and return.

Eight hours later he was home again, full of his day.

"Good time?"

"Sure! Fine! Couldn't have been a better change. . . ."

"From Giraud and de Gaulle, eh?"

"Matter of fact, on the way up this morning, we passed several units of French Moroccan infantry and cavalry, going through exercise drills. I didn't say anything, but I wouldn't be surprised if Giraud had got them out there on purpose so that I could see what he was talking about. . . ."

"You ride in the sedan all day?"

"Nope. They had a jeep for me, for the inspection of

the Second Armored and the Third Infantry. I must say, though, once in a jeep is enough to last quite a time."

"Look, are you supposed to be busy or anything? Because if . . ."

"Relax. Nobody's due to see me until dinnertime. Sit down. I want to tell you about it. I wish you could have seen the expression on the faces of some of those men in the infantry division. You could hear 'em say, 'Gosh—it's the old man himself!' " and Father roared with laughter.

"Where'd you eat, Pop?"

"In the field. With Mark Clark and Patton. And Harry, of course. Harry! . . . How'd you like that lunch in the field, hunh?"

From upstairs, where he was drawing a hot bath, Harry called back, "The luncheon music, that was the thing!"

"Oh, yes," said Father. "*Chattanooga Choo-Choo, Alexander's Rag-Time Band,* and that one about Texas, where they clap their hands, *you* know. . . ."

"*Deep in the Heart of Texas?*"

"That's right. And some waltzes. Elliott, tell me. Would any army in the world but the American Army have a regimental band playing songs like that while the Commander-in-Chief ate ham and sweet potatoes and green beans right near by? Hmmm?" He stretched. "Ah. I'm tired. Inspected the Ninth after lunch, and then drove on up to Port Lyautey."

"You see those ships there, in the harbor?"

"The ones we sank? Oh, sure."

"I didn't know you'd planned to go on up to Port Lyautey."

"We have a cemetery there," Father reminded me. "Eighty-eight Americans sleep up there. We left a wreath. . . . Left one in the French cemetery, too. . . ."

"Too bad it was such a poor day."

"Oh, it didn't start raining until around four-thirty. . . . Those troops, Elliott. They really look as if they're rarin' to go. Tough, and brown, and grinning, and . . . and *ready.*"

"Hey, what's that?"

"What? Oh, this? It's the messkit I ate lunch out of. They gave it to me. I thought I'd take it home as a souvenir."

"Honestly, Pop! You pick up and collect more stuff. . . . You realize, don't you, that the C-in-C of all the Armed Forces might just possibly be able to pick up a messkit at home?"

"Well. But I *ate* out of *this* one, at Rabat, the day I saw three divisions of American soldiers, who are fighting a tough war. It's a good souvenir. I'll take it home with me."

He had started back for his bedroom, to change his clothes, when there was a sudden bustle in the hall. In bounced Churchill, wreathed in smiles.

"Just in for a second," he cried. "Wanted to tell you the latest news. And good, for once."

"From headquarters?" asked Father. "What is it?"

"From London," said the P.M., beaming. "De Gaulle. It begins to look as though we'll be successful in persuading him to come down and join our talks."

There was a pause. Then: "Good," said Father shortly. He moved on slowly, toward his room. "Congratulations,

Winston. I always," he said, rather pointedly, "I always knew you'd be able to swing it."

That night, Father was in bed by nine-thirty. It was his longest night's rest since he had come to North Africa.

Friday, January 22

Just before noon the next day, some official Signal Corps pictures were taken of Father and the P.M., flanked by the Combined Chiefs of Staff. The sun was shining; everybody sat out on the terrace of Father's villa; there was laughter and easy, relaxed talk. The arduous part of the conference's work was nearing its end. There was still to be negotiated the tricky, deceptive business of arranging the compact between de Gaulle and Giraud, but all the foundation had been laid; for better or worse, the military decisions had—in broad—been taken, and there remained only the formulation of the communiqué announcing the Casablanca Conference to the world, and what it stood for.

After the picture-taking, Father lunched privately with General Marshall, and afterwards talked long with him in the living room of the villa. During their conversation, I was sitting quietly on the stairs just outside the door, waiting to be at hand in the event Father wanted anything. I could hear their talk: Marshall explaining the difficulties that the American Joint Chiefs had in forcing the issue for any invasion of Europe in 1943, now that we were committed to the Mediterranean; recapitulating the summary rejection of British ambitions for an adventure against Burma; reporting the combined agreement that any attack on Italy, in the event of a successful invasion of Sicily, should be very strictly limited in scope. After Marshall had left, during the afternoon, Father was to tell me that they had talked about the rocky path the Combined Chiefs had traveled to reach the plan for the invasion of Sicily; he was to complain, but philosophically, about the continuing British insistence on striking Europe from the south rather than from the west; he was to note his misgivings as to Stalin's attitude, when the news arrived of a further postponement of the invasion cross-channel; he was to comment that "Wars are uncertain affairs. To win this one, we must maintain a difficult unity with one ally by apparently letting another down. To win this war, we have been forced into a strategic compromise which will most certainly offend the Russians, so that later we will be able in turn to force a compromise which will most certainly offend the British. The compelling needs of war dictate a difficult course."

To which I started to comment, "But the war will be won—sooner or later. . . ."

And his answer: "The unity we have made for war is nothing to the unity we will have to build for peace. After the war—that's when the cry will come that our unity is no longer necessary. *That's* when the job will begin . . . in earnest."

No cocktails before dinner that night, and no wine with dinner. No pork. The Sultan, son of the true faith, was our guest.

He came with his young son, the Heir-Apparent, his Grand Vizier, and his Chief of Protocol, all clad magnificently in flowing white silk robes, and bearing gifts: two golden bracelets and a high golden tiara for Mother. One glimpse of the tiara, and Father gave me a straight-faced sidelong look, and then a solemn wink. The same thought was in both our minds: a picture of Mother presiding over a formal function at the White House with that imposing object perched atop her hair-do.

With the Sultan at Father's right and Churchill at his left, the dinner began. The P.M. began it in highest spirits—de Gaulle, he told us, had arrived that noon, had already lunched with Giraud, and had been to call at Mirador. But as the conversation proceeded, Churchill grew more and more disgruntled. What was the trouble? Father and the Sultan were animatedly chatting about the wealth of natural resources in French Morocco, and the rich possibilities for their development. They were having a delightful time, their French—not Mr. Churchill's strongest language—easily encompassing the question of the elevation of the living standards of the Moroccans and—the point—of how this would of necessity entail an important part of the country's wealth being retained within its own boundaries.

The Sultan expressed a keen desire to obtain the greatest possible aid in securing for his land modern educational and health standards.

Father pointed out that, to accomplish this, the Sultan should not permit outside interests to obtain concessions which would drain off the country's resources.

Churchill attempted to change the subject.

The Sultan, picking up the thread again, raised the question of what Father's advice would entail, insofar as the French government of the future was concerned.

Father, balancing his fork, remarked cheerfully enough that the postwar scene and the prewar scene would, of course, differ sharply, especially as they related to the colonial question.

Churchill coughed and again plunged into conversation along different lines.

Politely, the Sultan inquired more specifically, what did Father mean, "differ sharply"?

Father, dropping in a remark about the past relationship between French and British financiers combined into self-perpetuating syndicates for the purpose of dredging riches out of colonies, went on to raise the question of possible oil deposits in French Morocco.

The Sultan eagerly pounced on this; declared himself decidedly in favor of developing any such potentialities, retaining the income therefrom; then sadly shook his head as he deplored the lack of trained scientists and engineers among his countrymen, technicians who would be able to develop such fields unaided.

Churchill shifted uneasily in his chair.

Father suggested mildly that Moroccan engineers and scientists could of course be educated and trained under some sort of reciprocal educational program with, for instance, some of our leading universities in the United States.

The Sultan nodded. If it had been etiquette, he would have taken notes, names, and addresses of universities, right there on the spot.

Father pursued his point, toying with his water glass. He mentioned that it might easily be practicable for the Sultan to engage firms—American firms—to carry out the development program he had in mind, on a fee or percentage basis. Such an arrangement, he urged, would have the advantage of enabling the sovereign government of French Morocco to retain considerable control over its own resources, obtain the major part of any incomes flowing from such resources, and, indeed, eventually take them over completely.

Churchill snorted and tried not to listen.

It was a delightful dinner, everybody—with one exception—enjoying himself completely. As we rose from the table, the Sultan assured Father that, promptly on the heels of the war's close, he would petition the United States for aid in the development of his country. His face glowed. "A new future for my country!"

Glowering, biting at his cigar, Britain's Prime Minister followed the Sultan out of the dining room.

De Gaulle's arrival that day was, like heat lightning, nevertheless clearing the atmosphere. The Sultan obviously wanted to stay and discuss more specifically and with loving emphasis some of the points Father had raised during dinner, but Father's work for the evening was cut out for him. A signal to Captain McCrea, then, to stay and take notes; one to Robert Murphy and Harry Hopkins; one to me to hold myself in readiness to act as Ganymede—and all the others left. The stage was set for Charles de Gaulle.

He arrived ten minutes after the others had departed. He arrived with black clouds swirling around his high head, and with very poor grace. For some thirty minutes, he and Father talked, Father being charming, de Gaulle noncommittal. This is typical:

Father: "I am sure that we will be able to assist your great country in re-establishing her destiny."

De Gaulle: (*A wordless grunt.*)

Father: "And I assure you, it will be an honor for my country to participate in the undertaking."

De Gaulle: (*A grunt*) "It is nice of you to say so."

This wry colloquy at an end, the Frenchman unfolded his complete height from the chair where he had been stiffly angling it, and marched with formality and no backward glance to the door.

And a few moments later, in popped Churchill again, together with MacMillan. For another hour, they compared notes on the conversations each had had with de Gaulle. Father seemed unperturbed by the mighty sulk to which de Gaulle had treated him; I expect he simply acknowledged to himself that it squared with his preconceptions of the man. Murphy talked, then Churchill, then Harry, then Father's voice cutting in, then back to Churchill. I was thinking: What about the men and women inside France now? What about the men and women of the Resistance? Whose side are they on? De Gaulle's? Giraud's? Either's? On the side of both? What's the test? Who's right?

And Father's voice, quiet: "The past is the past, and it's done. We've nearly solved this thing now. These two: equal rank, equal responsibility in setting up the Provisional Assembly. When that's done, French democracy is reborn. When that Provisional Assembly starts to act, French democracy takes its first steps. Presently French democracy will be in a position to decide for itself what is to become of Giraud, or of de Gaulle. It will no longer be our affair."

And after Churchill and the others had left, in his bedroom, Father talked of France and her future.

"We've talked, the last few days," he said, "about gradually turning the civil control of France over to a joint Giraud-de Gaulle government, to administer as it is liberated. An interim control, to last only until free elections can again be held. It seems like a simple solution . . . but how de Gaulle will fight it!

"He's convinced, absolutely convinced that he should be the sole and arbitrary judge as to who shall or shall not participate in any provisional government!"

"He said something about French colonies, too, didn't he?" I put in. "I was just coming in from the pantry when I heard . . ."

"That's right. He made it quite clear that he expects the Allies to return all French colonies to French control immediately upon their liberation. You know, quite apart from the fact that the Allies will have to maintain military control of French colonies here in North Africa for months, maybe years, I'm by no means sure in my own mind that we'd be right to return France her colonies *at all, ever,* without first obtaining in the case of each individual colony some sort of pledge, some sort of statement of just exactly what was planned, in terms of each colony's administration."

"Hey, listen, Pop. I don't quite see this. I know the

colonies are important—but, after all they *do* belong to France . . . how come *we* can talk about not returning them?"

He looked at me. "*How* do they belong to France? Why does Morocco, inhabited by Moroccans, belong to France? Or take Indo-China. The Japanese control that colony now. Why was it a cinch for the Japanese to conquer that land? The native Indo-Chinese have been so flagrantly downtrodden that they thought to themselves: Anything must be better, than to live under French colonial rule! Should a land belong to France? By what logic and by what custom and by what historical rule?"

"Yes, but . . ."

"I'm talking about another war, Elliott," Father cried, his voice suddenly sharp. "I'm talking about what will happen to our world, if after *this* war we allow millions of people to slide back into the same semi-slavery!"

"And besides," I suggested, "we *should* have some say. We're the ones that are freeing France."

"Don't think for a moment, Elliott, that Americans would be dying in the Pacific tonight, if it hadn't been for the shortsighted greed of the French and the British and the Dutch. Shall we allow them to do it all, all over again? *Your* son will be about the right age, fifteen or twenty years from now."

"The United Nations—when they're organized—they could take over these colonies, couldn't they? Under a mandate, or as trustee—for a certain number of years."

"One sentence, Elliott. Then I'm going to kick you out of here. I'm tired. This is the sentence: When we've won the war, I will work with all my might and main to see to it that the United States is not wheedled into the position of accepting any plan that will further France's imperialistic ambitions, or that will aid or abet the British Empire in *its* imperial ambitions."

He pointed to the light switch, by the door, and jerked his thumb to the door itself.

Saturday, January 23

Harry Hopkins took care of a good many of Father's visitors, next morning, while Father slept late. General Arnold dropped by, and Averell Harriman, and General Patton. I was not needed for any of my minor chores, so I spent an hour or so looking through the library of books that our unknown and unknowing French hostess had put together. Her tastes ran to light fiction—novels by Colette, that sort of thing—but at length I ran across one item that caught my eye. It was a paper-backed book; I yanked it from the shelf and trotted into Father's bedroom, where he was just finishing a late breakfast.

"Ever read this?" I asked, tossing it to him.

It was André Maurois' biography of him. He crowed delightedly.

"Get me a pen, Elliott. There . . . on the dressing table."

And in his most florid French he inscribed a full-blown autograph, complete with grateful sentiments for the pleasant hours we had spent in this book's owner's home, addressing it to her with all the formal, high-flown phrases he could muster.

"Now stick it back on the shelf, Elliott. Bet she never

thinks to take it out again. Too bad: I'd like to see her face when and if she ever does."

"I'd like to see the expression on a bookseller's face, if he ever got a crack at buying this item."

"Don't be getting any ideas, now," he laughed. And back into the bookcase it went.

At lunch that afternoon there were just Harry, the P.M., Father, and I. And it was at that lunch table that the phrase "unconditional surrender" was born. For what it is worth, it can be recorded that it was Father's phrase, that Harry took an immediate and strong liking to it, and that Churchill, while he slowly munched a mouthful of food, thought, frowned, thought, finally grinned, and at length announced, "Perfect! And I can just see how Goebbels and the rest of 'em 'll squeal!"

"Goebbels and the rest of 'em" had been tentatively squealing for the past two or three days; in a pantry off the dining room, where the secret service agents used to sit and chat, there was a short-wave radio; we used to listen to their English language transmission: they were irritatedly speculating as to what was going on in Casablanca, and they were beginning to get closer and closer to the facts.

Father, once his phrase had been approved by the others, speculated about its effect in another direction.

"Of course, it's just the thing for the Russians. They couldn't want anything better. Unconditional surrender," he repeated, thoughtfully sucking a tooth. "Uncle Joe might have made it up himself."

And Harry said, "We'll get to work drawing up a draft of the statement right after lunch."

"Press'll be here tomorrow, Harry."

"I know. We'll have something in shape by the time the Combined Chiefs arrive at five-thirty."

Twice that afternoon Murphy and MacMillan dropped by, briefly, nervously. The critical appointment with both de Gaulle and Giraud was set for the next day. As the afternoon wore away, the Combined Chiefs of Staff arrived, to gather over the big table in the dining room with Father and the P.M. It was the last large-scale session of the conference; the last minor conflicts had been ironed out; a tentative date had been set for HUSKY; the P.M. made it clear that he expected Italy might be bypassed in favor of an onslaught on one side or other of the Balkan peninsula into Europe; ROUNDUP, the cross-channel invasion in 1943, had regretfully been set aside in favor of OVERLORD, the 1944 edition; plans had been set for a withdrawal of men and matériel to the United Kingdom just as soon as the Sicilian invasion had been secured (and the North African operation finally buttoned up). The meeting broke up around eight o'clock, with everyone in high spirits.

A first draft of the communiqué had been read, changes suggested, and the remains carted away to be reworked. Men could think of packing. The end of the conference was near.

No guests at dinner: just Harry, his son Bob (who had flown in begrimed and disheveled, two or three days earlier, from his front-line combat-photographer assignment), Father, and I. We might have played "Ghosts" during dinner, for all the talk there was of business.

After dinner, and on into the slender hours, Father and

the P.M. and Harry worked away at the final draft of the joint communiqué, and at the final draft of the cable to Stalin. Murphy and MacMillan sat in for a time, to lend any ideas they might have to that part of the communiqué which was to deal with the French political scene. They left together shortly after two; at two-thirty Churchill lifted his ever-ready glass in toast.

"Unconditional surrender." He put no exclamation point after it; there was only determination. We all drank.

Sunday, January 24

There was not much time left. At eleven the next morning, General Giraud arrived, and Father went straight to work.

"We must have your assurance, General, that you will sit down with de Gaulle and . . ."

"That man! He is a self-seeker."

"If I told you that I share with you some of your misgivings, and that this is precisely why I urge that you . . ."

"And a bad general. I need only support for the armies I can raise . . ."

". . . must sit down with him and work out a joint plan for the interim, provisional government of your country. Two such men as yourselves, General . . ."

Thirty minutes. At length:

"It is understood, M. le Président. It is understood."

While they talked, de Gaulle had arrived, and stood meantime, chafing, in the hall outside. They brushed past each other by the door. De Gaulle went in.

The ground had been paved, but the prima donna wanted urging. Like the girl in the story, he was playing hard to get. Father moved by degrees from charm to suasion to urgency to direct demand. It was at that point he nodded to me: I slipped out of the room, beckoned to Giraud, and we both went back in.

The generals looked at each other stiffly. All *bonhomie,* Father urged a handshake, to seal the compact they had individually made with him. Like two dogs, the two Frenchmen started almost to circle each other, and then exchanged a brief, reluctant handshake. In popped Churchill. Father was beaming. He didn't say, "Tell the man . . . go on, tell him what you've told me," but that was in his expression.

"We have agreed," said de Gaulle shortly, to the P.M., "we have agreed that we will do our best to work out a satisfactory plan of action"—he paused—"together."

Giraud nodded in confirmation.

"Come on," cried Father. "Pictures!" And the four of them went out to the terrace in back, to have their pictures taken. While the shutters clicked, and the motion-picture cameras turned over, the two generals shook hands again. And Father heaved a great sigh.

It was just after noon when the newspaper correspondents and photographers who had been gathering outside for some time were invited to sit on the lawn. Side by side, Father and Churchill sat and talked of the conference. The hollows under Father's eyes, his black tie and crêpe on his sleeve (he was still in mourning at that time for Grannie's death) were the only spots lacking in color, under the brilliant sun. The P.M.'s homburg was perched jauntily on his head, his cigar swiveled from side to side; he was in fine fettle. "Unconditional surrender": the correspondents' pencils jotted down swift notes.

It was not a lengthy press conference; at its end, the President and the Prime Minister shook hands all around. "You're an élite group," Father murmured; "a routine press conference in the White House always means too many to shake hands with."

And then he and I were inside again, in his room, to say goodbye, for I was heading back to my unit in a very few minutes.

"Well?"

"Well?"

"Okay, I'd say, Pop . . . okay!"

"Yes . . . we got quite a lot done. Well worth it."

"And I think it was a good change for you."

"Like to check one impression with you, Elliott. I'd like to know just one thing."

"What?"

"I'm anxious to know . . ." He trailed off, and then began again. "You see, what the British have done, down through the centuries, historically, is the same thing. They've chosen their allies wisely and well. They've always been able to come out on top, with the same reactionary grip on the peoples of the world and the markets of the world, through every war they've ever been in."

"Yes. . . ."

"*This* time, *we're* Britain's ally. And it's right we should be. But . . . first at Argentia, later in Washington, now here at Casablanca . . . I've tried to make it clear to Winston—and the others—that while we're their allies, and in it to victory by their side, they must never get the idea that we're in it just to help them hang on to the archaic, medieval Empire ideas."

"I know what you mean," I said slowly. "I think they got the idea."

"I hope they did. I hope they realize they're not senior partner; that we're not going to sit by, after we've won, and watch their system stultify the growth of every country in Asia and half the countries in Europe to boot. . . .

"Great Britain signed the Atlantic Charter. I hope they realize the United States government means to make them live up to it."

Harry had stuck his head in the door. "Nogues is here, to give you a goodbye. And Michelier, too."

"Michelier?"

"The Commander-in-Chief of the French North African Fleet."

"Oh, yes. Be right out. . . . Well, son?"

"Goodbye, Pop."

"Goodbye."

"Say hello to Mother, give her a kiss for me, and take good care of yourself."

". . . And don't forget to take good care of *yourself*, too. *You're* the one who could get hurt."

Twenty minutes later he was on his way, with his motorcade. And I was heading back to Algiers and the war.

5

FROM CASABLANCA TO CAIRO

THE NEWS OF STALINGRAD was a tonic for all of us in Algiers. And for the next few months, my outfit had enough grueling hard work so that we could put up with a tonic every now and then. As though it were not enough work simply to supply all the information required by the strategic air forces in their bombing raids over Italy, while keeping tabs for the tactical air forces on the Nazi troops and air support in front of our ground troops in Africa, we had now in addition to take on the job of photographic reconnaissance for HUSKY, the invasion of Sicily. Just a word about this: to map an objective from the air means maintaining straight flight-lines and set altitudes, so that all your pictures will be to the same scale; it means flying in a stripped-down ship that carries no guns for defense; it denies the pilot opportunity for evasive flying; to sum up, it ain't fun. We were losing planes at the rate of twenty per cent per month. Within ninety days of our arrival in North Africa, of the original ninety-four pilots in my outfit there were less than ten per cent to answer roll call.

So with conditions like those to operate under, my nose was pretty close to the grindstone through the spring and early summer. Once or twice I was invited over to General Eisenhower's headquarters to play bridge, generally with Harry Butcher and "Tex" Lee, the General's naval and military aides. (When I drew Ike as my partner, I was on the winning side; if not, I had to depend on luck.)

The last of those bridge dates came a few days before we hit Sicily. I was feeling pretty good because of the part my outfit had played in the capture—strictly by the air forces—of the island fortress of Pantelleria. Perky about the job we'd done, I was in a mood to invite the Nazi to "bring 'em on—we'll take all you got!" General Ike gave me one of those steady, calculating looks.

"Pantelleria, hmmm?"

"First time in history ground forces have ever surrendered to air forces," I crowed. "We ought to be able to move in anywhere in Europe we want, now."

"When we move in on Europe," General Eisenhower said, soberly, "we'll have such superiority of matériel and firepower that nobody'll be able to stop us. And," he added, "we won't move in on Europe until then. The only thing is," he said, suddenly thoughtful, "even then, we may be stopped."

There was silence for a few moments, all of us thinking about the French coast, and men getting killed, planes being shot down, ships being sunk.

"Europe's still a lot of miles and a lot of months away,"

said the General, thinking out loud. "First things first. Sicily's first."

I knew General Eisenhower had urged a second front in 1942, and had his ideas rejected by the British. I knew he had agreed with the Joint Chiefs of Staff that there should be a second front in Europe in 1943, although the British were more easily able to dissuade their American opposites this second time, since we were already so heavily committed in the Mediterranean theater. Now, listening to this sober and humble appraisal in the early summer of 1943, I conceived a higher regard for our American commander—for his care, his concern for men, his insistence on the biggest edge American production could give our armies. I could guess that even in the spring of 1944, when I was certain the invasion of western Europe must surely come, General Eisenhower would—even though committed heart and soul—still approach the job with humility and the most cautious sort of confidence.

Then HUSKY; and the preparatory work our outfit had done made us all feel pretty good. Our troops were in the process of cleaning up the last Nazis in Sicily when, late in July, from the War Department to my commanding general came a request that I be sent back to the States, to consult on questions of reorganization of reconnaissance operations. At the same time, from the Pacific theater was coming Colonel Karl Polifka, who had been doing work similar to mine. The request meant two months' assignment in Washington, August and September; and while I regretted leaving my command still I looked forward to seeing Father and Mother and the rest of the family—those of them who were not overseas on duty.

The work I had in the Pentagon was absorbing and bore importantly on our future reconnaissance operations but, fortunately for me, it was not so exacting but what I had several opportunities to chat with Father.

He was not looking as well as I would have liked to find him: he had aged perceptibly, even since Casablanca, six months before; that summer he was, in addition, having a recurrence of his sinus trouble; but his spirits were high. He exuded a wonderfully calm confidence about the military aspects of the war. I used to find time to drop in on him either just after he had finished breakfast, in the morning, from around nine until ten, or late in the evening, after his last caller had left, around eleven. In his mind, the strategy of war was developed to the point where he could see final victory, and even put a date on it. One night in September he mentioned such dates.

"In Europe, by the end of 1944."

I whistled.

"Look at the way the Red Army is plowing through center . . ."

"But the end of 1944!"

"If we're able to hit France hard enough, and swiftly enough, sure."

"France?" I asked, slyly.

He was imperturbable. "I don't know," he said. "France would be logical. It might as easily be the Lowlands. Or Germany. Or Norway. I don't know." His face was absolutely straight.

"What about Japan? That island-hopping—it's taking time. . . . Say, by the end of '46?"

"Nope. Latter part of 1945. Early 1946, at the latest. Goodness, when Hitler is knocked out, and we're able to pour everything we've got at Japan—*everything*, I say—what chance do they stand?"

"And what about the British? And the Russians? Will they be helping us? Or just sitting back, licking their wounds?"

"You know the statement at Casablanca. Churchill agreed to it, and so did Stalin, later."

"From what I know of the British, they're going to be pretty damn sick of the war, after Hitler's beaten. And can we trust the Russians?"

"We're trusting them now, aren't we? What reason have we for not trusting them tomorrow? Anyway . . . I hope to be seeing Stalin himself, pretty soon."

"*What?* Really?"

He nodded. "Right at the moment, we're dickering. He wants us to meet him in his own country, on his own stamping-grounds. He's still careful to point out that he is personally in charge of the Red Army. And I must say, so long as the Red Army keeps on doing what it's doing, it's difficult for anyone to suggest anything which might slow it up."

"I imagine he's a little scared, too."

"Scared? Of what?"

"Oh, that you and Churchill will gang up on him. Something like that."

Father chuckled. "I suspect his people are pretty

much aware of how *friendly* my relations with Winston are," he said, somewhat enigmatically.

A very few days later, Father and a group of his advisers took a train north for another meeting with the British Prime Minister and their chiefs of staff, at Quebec. This was the conference which was code-named QUADRANT, and I was unable to attend it in any capacity, by reason of my air forces assignment, which took me, during the month of August, out to California—to various manufacturing plants and the airfield at Muroc Dry Lake—three or four times, working on special reconnaissance problems. But Father had told me in advance about it; I even was familiar—though vaguely—with the agenda. So in the last part of August, when he had returned from Quebec, I asked him how the Great Debate was going.

"Well," he said, "it begins to look as though the debate is over. The British have been working on a plan for the cross-channel invasion—it's got a lot of question marks, to hear George Marshall on the subject—but the plan has at least been drawn up. And it's been approved." He smiled ruefully. "Winston insisted on our approving it—'in principle.' Just so the back door can be left open."

I said something to the effect that if he could only arrange his meeting with Stalin he would not lack for a helping hand in convincing the British of the need for a western front.

A week or so later, that subject came up again, in a roundabout sort of way. Father had indicated to me that, whatever his confidence in the strictly military aspects of the war, the political considerations left something to be desired. The structure of peace had been taking more specific form in his mind, necessarily, and its demands were leading him to the same plans for a meeting with the other world leaders.

"The United Nations . . . They aren't that yet, completely, but they're getting there, and they can be pushed a lot farther along. At the moment . . . !"

"What's the matter? I should say it wasn't so bad. . . . At least we're all working in the same direction."

He pushed aside a heap of papers (we were in his study, on the second floor of the White House; it was close on midnight) and began doodling on a pad. "The trouble is," he said, "we're not really headed in the same direction, except on the surface. Take Chiang Kai-shek. With all the difficulties that face him, there's still little excuse for the fact that his armies are not fighting the Japanese.

"War is too political a thing. Depending on how desperate are a country's straits, she is likely to wage war only in such a way as will benefit her politically in the long run, rather than fighting to end the war as swiftly as possible."

"Whom are you thinking of, Pop? China? Britain?"

He nodded. "Even our alliance with Britain," he went on, "holds dangers of making it seem to China and Russia that we support wholly the British line in international politics. . . ." He concentrated on his doodle: it was a big number "4," very fancy. "The United States will have to *lead*," he said. "Lead . . . and use our good offices always to conciliate, help to solve the differences which will arise between the others—between Russia and England, in Europe; between the British Empire and China and between China and Russia, in the Far East. We will be able to do that," he went on, "because we're big, and we're strong, and we're self-sufficient. Britain is on the decline, China—still in the eighteenth century. Russia—suspicious of us, and making us suspicious of her. America is the only great power that can make peace in the world stick.

"It's a tremendous responsibility. And the only way we can start living up to it is by getting to talk with these men, face-to-face."

"How about that? Heard from Uncle Joe again?"

"Yes. Any time Winston and I want to come to Moscow, it's fine with Stalin."

In mid-September, then, we were as far from a meeting of the Big Four as we were in January.

The last time I had a chance to talk to Father, I had to trick him into talking. It was after breakfast; he was still in bed; the day outside was chill and wet with a September rain, and he was not feeling up to par. He made me do the talking at first, by interesting himself in my work, and asking me questions about it. He wanted to know about how night reconnaissance had worked out: I had flown the initial, experimental missions over Sicily, and I told him about the dodges we had worked out for getting a good look at Nazi night-time troop movements; how we had used flash bombs, dropped thirty seconds apart, which went off two-thirds of the way down, and lighted up a square mile around, affording us magnificent opportunities for getting pictures of the enemy on the move. At length, I contrived to maneuver the conversation to my hopes that the job would be over soon, and to questions as to what might be in the wind that would indicate there was progress on the political front.

"We may be able to swing the meetings I told you about, Elliott," he said. "It's pretty definite that there will have to be two of them: one with Chiang and a second with Uncle Joe. Those two can't meet together, when there is a first-rate Japanese army standing ready on Stalin's Siberian borders—and while Russia still hasn't declared war against Japan."

I asked if the chances looked better of being able to get Stalin to a meeting on neutral ground.

"I think they are. I think they are. If so . . ."

"Yes?"

"If so, it'll probably be somewhere in your direction."

That was what I had been waiting for. It meant that maybe I would be able to get the assignment again to act as Father's aide. With that news, it was not so difficult to say goodbye at the end of September. I hung on to the hope that in not too many months, I would be seeing him again, somewhere around the Mediterranean.

Back with my outfit, we made immediate plans to advance our headquarters from La Marsa, a resort village a few miles from Tunis, up to the southern end of the Italian boot. By November we were established in San Severo, chipping away at the tough German defenses and cussing at the hideous weather that too infrequently gave us a chance to get at the enemy from the air. The fact that Italy was knocked out of the war by then, and the rocking the Nazi had taken on the Russian steppes all summer and fall hadn't done his morale any good; but on the other hand, Allied morale was not so high, in Italy, as our machine stumbled down to a crawl, and our men in the ground forces had the dispiriting experience of having to look practically right into the mouths of the 88's the Nazi had sprinkled all through the Italian mountain passes.

November got colder, and the weather got worse. Sunny Italy was the wriest joke anybody wanted to make. And I wondered what was to become of Father's hopes for a Big Three or Big Four meeting. And then, suddenly, I got a secret communication from General Smith, Eisenhower's Chief-of-Staff. I was to proceed immediately to Oran to meet "an important personage." That could only mean the meeting I had been waiting for.

The afternoon of the 19th of November I flew back across the Mediterranean to Oran, and was promptly driven to join General Eisenhower at his temporary headquarters. I found that my brother Franklin had been given leave from duty on his destroyer; it had been nearly a year since I had seen him. This time Father was not flying; he was aboard the big new battleship *Iowa;* I imagine she was just about making the Rock of Gibraltar at the moment when I was making myself comfortable with Franklin over a highball, in Oran.

There was considerable brass around and about: besides General Eisenhower there were the British Admiral Cunningham, our own Vice Admiral Hewitt, and assorted brigadiers and commodores—as well as good old Mike Reilly, who had again preceded the President on his trip in order to keep his watchful eye on everybody. I do not suppose that Mike would have looked at his own grandmother without a little suspicion; he always took his job of guarding the President as conscientiously as could be.

Saturday morning we were all up early. It was a clear, bright, crisp day, for which we were grateful after the drizzle of Friday. By eight-thirty we were all down dockside at Oran's naval base, Mers-el-Kebir; and through binoculars we watched someone being lowered into the *Iowa's* motor whaleboat.

Twenty minutes later he waved us a big hello, and grinned a healthy, sea-tanned grin at us. "Roosevelt weather!" he cried.

Then into General Ike's car—Father, the General, Franklin Junior, and I—and we started on the fifty-mile drive to La Senia airport, snaking along steep mountain roads. The sea voyage had done Father good; he looked fit; and he was filled with excited anticipation of the days ahead. Cairo, he told us, and after that Teheran. First to meet with Chiang, and then with Uncle Joe. He was full of his intentions.

"The war—and the peace," he said, and there was thankfulness in his voice. "Can you wait, Ike?"

"Just about, sir."

Franklin and I plied him with questions of home, of Mother, of our sister, Anna. He had brought newspapers again, he told us; we would have a crack at them that night, if there was time. There were familiar faces in his party, and some new ones too: besides Harry Hopkins, General Watson, Admiral Brown, and Admiral McIntire, Admiral Leahy had come along for this conference. Beyond a few perfunctory remarks about the country we passed through, and a few words of home, Father found it difficult to talk of anything but the days ahead. We were at La Senia in what seemed like no time, and at once Father got aboard his C-54. Major Otis Bryan was again his pilot; Franklin, Harry Hopkins, and the braid and the brass joined him; and they took off at once for Tunis.

I had my own plane at La Senia, a B-25 night photographic reconnaissance plane; and one of my squadron commanders, Major Leon Gray, was there to accompany me. We had a few minutes of anxiety when one of the engines would not act properly, but finally, thirty minutes after the official plane had taken off, we were airborne; we set our engines a little higher than usual, and beat them to El Aouina after all.

Once more General Ike, Franklin, and I rode with Father from the airport to the villa prepared for him at Carthage (Oh, here it comes again: the villa was known as the "White House"). Our road ran by the ruined amphitheater at Carthage; it was the first time Father had ever been in this part of the world; nothing would do but we must stop and have a look at the ruins.

Father's villa, right on the shore of the Gulf of Tunis, was a lovely place, and he settled into it expansively. On the way through Carthage, I had bethought myself that the rear headquarters of my outfit, base for nearly half my units, was at La Marsa, right near by. It was too good a chance to be missed.

"Would you, Pop?"

"What's that?"

"Inspect my units at La Marsa?"

"Sure! When? Could we tuck it in later this afternoon? Say around five o'clock?"

I laughed. "I hope I can have everything ready by then. I'll try." And I hurried over to my headquarters to organize a review and inspection. At that time, I commanded the Northwest African Photo Reconnaissance Wing, which was made up of some six thousand Allied troops—about twenty-eight hundred of them stationed here, the rest in southern Italy. Leon Gray, Frank Dunn (my second-in-command), and I hustled everything into as apple-pie order as we could, while back in Carthage Father was working over the official mail that had been delivered from Washington on his arrival at Oran.

By five-thirty my men were drawn up, looking pretty elegant, we had to admit. Father, from a jeep, reviewed the entire complement.

"See the uniforms, Pop? We've got a regular United Nations, right here."

"Americans, of course. French, British, Canadians . . . what's that uniform?"

"South African. And there are New Zealanders and Australians, too."

"Looks like a fine outfit, Elliott. You should be proud."

"Don't worry. I am."

Dinner was a party, with Kay Somersby, General

Eisenhower's chauffeur, and Nancy Gatch, Admiral Gatch's daughter, who was doing Red Cross work in North Africa, gracing the table. Father had thought to leave Tunis first thing in the morning, but the General promptly scotched that.

"A night flight, Sunday night, would be better, sir. Getting you to Cairo in the morning."

"A night flight? Why? I particularly wanted to get a view of the road the battle took, from El Alamein."

"Too risky, sir. We don't want to have to run fighter escort all the way to Cairo; it'd just be asking for trouble. Quite apart from that, the night flight is a much smoother trip."

"But . . ."

"The night flight is s.o.p., sir."

"Standard operating procedure, Pop," I put in.

"*Thank* you," said Father, elaborately. "There are a few *bits* of Army slang with which the Commander-in-Chief *is* familiar." And then, turning to the General, "Okay, Ike. You're the boss. But I get something in return."

"What's that, sir?"

"If you're going to make me stay over at Carthage all Sunday, you've got to take me on a personally conducted tour of the battlefields—ancient and modern."

"That's a bargain, sir."

My duties at La Marsa kept me from accompanying Father on that personally conducted tour, but Franklin sat on the jump seat in front of General Ike and Father, and that night he told me about it. Father had grilled Ike pretty closely, not only on the war that had been fought to a breakthrough by the Allies at Medjez-el-Bab and at Tebourba, but also on the wars that the Carthaginians had fought in antiquity. The fact that Ike knew the details of each conflict backward and forward pleased Father hugely: it showed that Ike, like Father, had a bent for history, and a love of knowledge. Franklin told me Father was beaming by the time they got back to the villa. Just as Ike had been about to climb out of the car, back by the "White House," Father had put a restraining hand on his arm.

"You know, Ike—I'm afraid I'm going to have to do something to you you won't like."

Franklin had pricked up his ears. What was this? Canning him from his theater command? Or sarcasm: promoting him on the spot to some new and bigger command?

"I know what Harry Butcher is to you, Ike," Father had said. Ike had nodded. "Well, despite the fact that he's your right arm—anyway, your left—I may have to take him away from you."

Ike's face had clouded over, just a shade. "Well, sir . . ."

"The point is, Elmer Davis has turned in his resignation again. What would you say if I drafted 'Butch' to take over the job?"

"Well, Mr. President—I won't pretend it wouldn't be tough. But if you need him, if you give the word, the answer is, sure, go ahead."

Father had paused, with what Franklin reported to me as a very satisfied look on his face. It was the sort of answer he liked, and he was bound to like Eisenhower the more for it, especially inasmuch as he knew what losing Butcher would mean to the General.

"I'll see, Ike. Maybe it won't be necessary. I'll let you know. If you mention it to Butch, be sure and tell him that he was Elmer's own choice for the job. In any case, it won't be definite till January."

I'm sure that Butch was delighted when—two months later—it was decided that Elmer Davis would stay on the job.

By the time I got back to his villa that night, before dinner, Father was full of two subjects. He was lambasting the Congressmen who were making it difficult for the country to fight the war with vim and virulence. That night several sets of ears must have burned, back in Washington, not least among them those of Vandenberg, Taft, "Pappy" O'Daniel, and Ham Fish. His other subject was his consuming interest in his trip of the afternoon. He had seen an Arab tribe on the move, with its camel caravan; he had seen the dozens of burned-out tanks and trucks that were strewn all over the recent battlefields; and he had had a good long look at Hill 609, that unimpressive pimple of land where a lot of our men were killed, and where the American soldiers had come of age.

At dinner that night it was Leahy, dour and quiet, Father's aides, Brown and Pa Watson, Admiral McIntire, and Franklin and myself. Franklin and I, we each knew, would be unable to go to Cairo with Father: Franklin was due back on his destroyer, and I had more work ahead of me at La Marsa. But we drove down to El Aouina nonetheless, to see Father and his party off.

Harry Hopkins joined our party at the field; there were two berths in the plane that had been earmarked for him and Father.

Just before Father's plane took off, he renewed an argument he had started with Franklin Junior on Saturday: why wasn't Franklin going to come on to Cairo there and then? But my brother just grinned, and waved goodbye, and the big C-54 took off around ten-thirty. On the way back to Carthage, Franklin told me about the argument: his destroyer, the *Mayrant,* had been shot up at Palermo; some German bombers had got lucky and dumped two very-close misses and a hit on her; she was headed out of Gibraltar in a few days, on the long and dangerous trip back to a stateside Navy yard for repairs. And Franklin simply wanted no part of a proposition that meant that he, as the *Mayrant's* executive officer, would not go along on a voyage involving danger for the rest of the crew.

There was a day's and a night's job to be done at my rear headquarters; Tuesday night I reported to General Eisenhower, in whose plane I was to fly east to Cairo. Besides myself, there were General Ike, a half-dozen or so of his staff officers, and my brother-in-law, Major John Boettiger, down from Italy where he was attached to the Allied Military Government. We took off in the General's C-54 from Tunis after dark; with the dawn we were approaching Egypt; by mid-morning we were circling over the ATC airfield at Cairo.

I was about to begin my third wartime conference.

6

CAIRO I

THAT NIGHT, AS WE FLEW over the wide stretch of desert from Tunis toward Egypt, I could hear my brother-in-law talking to General Eisenhower, for a time, discussing with him in terms of mild complaint the difficulties which the military government officers in Italy were faced with. At length I slept, awaking in time to watch our approach to Cairo.

It is a spectacular sight. For hundreds of miles the desert reaches out, an expanse of unredeemed brown. Then, quite suddenly and unexpectedly, there is the greenest of green, so bright it makes you blink. This is the strip of rich earth running north and south, the thin ribbon of land irrigated by the Nile. We craned our necks briefly to catch a glimpse of the pyramids at Gizeh and "Where's the Sphinx? Is that it?" and then our plane was dipping down toward the green, banking in a curve over the muddy blue of the Nile, and on to Payne Field, the ATC field southeast of the city. There were Army cars waiting to take us back across the Nile again, through the crowded streets of Cairo, and on out beyond to the suburb of Mena west of the city, where the conference had already been going on for two days.

As at Casablanca, Mike Reilly and his men had seen to it that barbed wire was flung up around the area designated for the conference. Most of the participants were quartered in the Mena House, a hotel that had been designed by a mid-Victorian architect, from the look of it. Father was staying at Ambassador Kirk's villa; Churchill and the Chiangs, both of whom had arrived the evening before Father got there, were also put up in villas near by. I imagine that Mike did a lot of worrying during the Cairo Conference, despite the barbed wire; to his way of thinking, Cairo was simply a city filled with a lot of people whose political quirks might lead them to think kindly of assassinating any or all the principals living in near-by Mena.

As soon as the Army car had dropped me off at Ambassador Kirk's villa, I went directly in to say a good morning to Father. It was not yet ten-thirty; he was still in bed, breakfasting alone. He looked well and rested. I asked him what had been happening.

"Happening? A lot. A lot."

"Like what?"

"Oh . . . I've met the Generalissimo, taken a trip out to look at the Pyramids, gotten a radiogram from Uncle Joe . . ."

"What's that? Saying what?"

"Saying that he'd be at Teheran on the twenty-eighth. Next Sunday."

"Then the meeting is definitely on."

"It would seem so." He forked some eggs into his mouth and winked at me.

"What do you think of the Generalissimo?"

He shrugged. "About what I'd expected, I guess. He and Madame Chiang were here for dinner last night—stayed until around eleven. He knows what he wants, and he knows he can't have it all. But we'll work out something." He shifted the tray out of his way. "Give me your hand, will you, Elliott?" He swung himself out of bed, and started dressing. As he dressed, he talked, while I stole some toast from the tray and poured myself some coffee.

"There've been two full meetings, so far. Complete with the Combined Chiefs. But at those meetings . . . I guess they were too formal. What has really been going on, in China and Burma and India, didn't come out. I learned more just talking to the Chiangs last night than I did from more than four hours of meeting with the Combined Chiefs."

"More about what?"

"More about the war that *isn't* being fought, and why. Chiang's troops aren't fighting at all—despite the reports that get printed in the papers. He claims his troops aren't trained, and have no equipment—and that's easy to believe. But it doesn't explain why he's been trying so hard to keep Stilwell from training Chinese troops. And it doesn't explain why he keeps thousands and thousands of his best men up in the northwest—up on the borders of Red China."

Arthur Prettyman, Father's valet, came in, took away the tray, and presently came back again to help Father.

Father went on talking. He spoke of the difficulties of supply, and of the resistance the British had been putting up to the building of the Ledo Road . . . of the British reluctance to mount any offensives through the Burmese jungle . . . of the problems connected with flying supplies over the Hump, and the tragic cost of that particular logistical task. I had talked with plenty of ATC fliers who knew conditions in the CBI theater from the inside out, and knew they had plenty to beef about, and I said so. Father listened, nodding.

"It's no fun, an assignment out there," he said. "I've heard people talking about the Pacific theater being a forgotten theater. Compared to CBI, the Pacific is at Times Square, at Broadway and Forty-second Street. I don't envy anybody out there, from Stilwell on down. They've got the job of fighting as big a war as they can, with next to no supplies. You can't blame them for paying no attention to the fact that the main war at the moment is in Europe, and that as soon as the war in Europe is won the center of gravity will swing in the direction of Japan and the Philippines. It will never swing in their direction, but they can't be blamed for trying to make it swing there.

"I saw Stilwell the other night, at the staff meeting. I asked him to be sure and save some time when the two of us can have a chat, by ourselves. I can't think what would be happening in China, if it weren't for him.

"Actually, of course, the job in China can be boiled down to one essential: China must be kept in the war, tieing up Japanese soldiers."

I asked about the British in the CBI. "I thought big

stuff was going to start when Mountbatten got out there."

Father smiled. "I guess Mountbatten did too," he said. "What he's anxious to do now is get hold of enough landing-craft to stage an amphibious attack on the Andaman Islands."

"The Andaman Islands? Where are *they*?"

"To hear Churchill talk, you'd think they were the most strategic point this side of his beloved Balkans. Oh, they're in the Bay of Bengal, off southern Burma. From the Andamans, they figure they'd be able to attack Rangoon."

"I take it any landing-craft available are being reserved for the second front, next spring."

"Believe it or not, Elliott, the British are raising questions and doubts again about that western front."

"About OVERLORD? But I thought that was all settled at Quebec!"

"So did we all. It is, too. It's settled. But Winston keeps on making his doubts clear to everybody."

"Has he said why?"

"It's still the idea of an attack through the Balkans. 'A common front with the Russians,' that sort of thing. General Marshall is . . . very patient, very polite, and very firm. I think Winston is beginning not to like George Marshall very much. He finds that no matter what tactics he uses, whether it's wheedling or logic or anger, Marshall still likes best the strategy of hitting Hitler an uppercut right on the point of the jaw."

"I wouldn't envy anybody the job of standing up to the P.M."

"Well, I'll tell you one man," said Father, "one man

who deserves a medal for being able to get along with him. And that's Ike Eisenhower."

"Say!" I cried. "That reminds me!"

"What?" asked Father. "And hurry up, because I'm due for a session with the Combined Chiefs at eleven. That's in five minutes."

"Are you serious about Ike deserving a medal?"

"Sure I am. But he won't take one. At the same time MacArthur was given the Medal of Honor, it was offered to Ike, and he turned it down. Said it was given for valor, and he hadn't done anything valorous."

"I was talking with Beedle Smith," I said, "a month or so ago. And he said that there *was* one medal Ike *did* want. The Legion of Merit. He said Ike had told him once that it was the only medal he didn't have that he really wanted. The thing he likes about it, Smith said, is that it's a medal that anybody can get, even if it's only for being a damn good Army cook. But Ike's never gotten it."

Father thought for a second, smiling. "Could we keep it a secret?"

"I don't know why not."

"Good. If you can get a message through to Smith, asking him to draw up a citation—North African campaign, Sicilian campaign, all that—and if he can get a medal here on time, I'll pin it on him myself, before we leave for Teheran."

"I'll get right on it," I said.

And while Father went on to his meeting with the Combined Chiefs, I went upstairs to the room that had been made ready for me, washed, and then set about promoting a real breakfast. It was served up on the terraced roof of Ambassador Kirk's villa, an extremely pleasant, sunny spot with a commanding view of the Pyramids, just a good spit away. This luxury reminded me that things at Cairo were going to be different from the way they were at Casablanca: for to this conference the Navy had supplied eight chief stewards and chief cooks, Filipinos, wonderfully efficient both at producing quite respectable banquets out of Army chow and at watchfully taking care of everybody's last need. This meant, for example, that I was not needed to fill empty highball glasses for those that wanted a drink. It meant that I did not need, while still acting as Father's aide, to be on tap every second of the time, and at each appointment. It meant that I would have a freer time, and would even be able to get away from the villa on occasion and see what was going on elsewhere.

That sunny morning on the roof, I was able to relax thoroughly, look idly at the Pyramids, and reflect—as I imagine everyone seeing them has done—on time and eternity, on the wars that had swirled past these tombs, the generals that had come and gone, the Pharaohs, the Caesars and the kings and the field marshals and generalissimos.

Admiral McIntire, Father's physician, came along to disturb (thank goodness) this last-cup-of-coffee reverie. He was worried about Father's projected flight to Teheran.

"How can you worry about anything in this sunshine, Mac?"

"I'm serious, Elliott. I think he should fly only as far as Basra and then go on from there by train. Those mountains in Iran—he'll have to go up pretty high. And the altitude . . ."

"There must be some mountain passes."

"Even so. . . . You're having lunch with him, aren't you?"

"As far as I know I am."

"He'll listen to you. Tell him you think he ought to finish the trip by train, will you? I'm serious."

"Have you spoken to Otis Bryan?"

"No."

"Why don't I ask him to look into it, see whether there aren't some mountain passes? How high can Father fly safely?"

"Nothing over seven thousand five hundred. And that's tops."

"Okay. I'll speak to Bryan. He's flown Father around enough so that he'll understand the problem. Forget about it, Mac. I'll take care of it."

The conference downstairs broke up just before one. I went down to say hello to the Prime Minister and to Harry Hopkins, and to see the others I had not seen since Casablanca—General Marshall, General Arnold, Admiral King, General Somervell, and their British opposites. For a few moments before we went in to lunch I had a chance to chat with Father. I asked him how it looked for OVERLORD.

"Very 'iffy,'" he smiled. "At least, from the British point of view. The plans drawn at Quebec are still the plans, though." He started to break off for a moment, then continued, "They've introduced the idea of a smaller attack, perhaps on Norway, with the weight continuing in the Mediterranean. But it's not over yet." He nodded in Marshall's direction, with a meaningful look in his eye. "General George," he said, "is still the best man at the conference table. As far as he's concerned, the only question open for discussion is: Who will be in command of our invasion from the west?"

Harry Hopkins and John Boettiger moved over then, from another group, and Father went out with them to sit in the garden until lunchtime. At the lunch table, there were few references to business; Harry did remind Father that the Chiangs were giving a cocktail party that afternoon.

"Say, that's right! And I'll never be able to go. Elliott . . . that one's for you. How about it?"

"Cocktail party at the Chiangs? Sure, if you don't need me for anything else."

"This afternoon," Father said, "there won't be much except some protocol visits. Stick around and help keep my visitors happy until their appointments. But knock off at four-thirty or so and drive over to the Chiangs' villa."

"What excuses shall I offer?"

"For me? Laurence Steinhardt has an appointment with me at five o'clock."

At that time Steinhardt was our Ambassador to Turkey, and there had been considerable speculation about Turkey's entry into the war on the side of the Allies. I asked Father if any decision had been taken yet.

"No final decision has been agreed on," he said. "But my mind is made up."

Harry Hopkins chuckled. You could tell that this subject was one on which they had talked before, and that there was disagreement on the final decision from some other, third, party. Nor was it difficult to guess that the third party was the P.M.

"Is *your* decision on Turkey top-secret around here, Pop?"

He laughed. "I've told about everybody, I guess," he said. "Turkey'll come in the war on our side only in the event she's given a lot of Lend-Lease equipment. What does she want it for? Just so she can be strong in the postwar world? Winston thinks she should be given the equipment and come in to the fight. Why? When Lend-Lease equipment to Turkey means less equipment for the invasion of Europe, why does he think so?"

"Maybe Turkey on our side would strengthen his argument to fight Hitler from the Mediterranean," I guessed.

"It *could* be," said Father sarcastically.

After lunch, what Father had referred to as "the protocol visits" began, and Ambassador Kirk's villa took on the appearance of the Grand Central Station during rush hour. On our own version of an assembly line, we greeted visitors in the front hall, escorted them into the living room, made sure they had smokes, chatted with them a few moments, and at the properly designated time and on signal, ushered them out into the garden, where Father was sitting, sometimes with Harry, sometimes with me, sometimes with Pa Watson, his military aide. In order, reading from two-fifteen until after four-thirty, they were: Sir Ahmed Mohammed Hassenein Pasha, Chief of the Egyptian Royal Cabinet; Mustapha Nahas Pasha, Egyptian Prime Minister and Minister of Foreign Affairs (who presented the regrets of H. M. King Farouk I, who had been hurt in a recent automobile accident and could not come to call in person); H. M. King George of Greece (Father said, "Charming fellow, considering what an empty head!"); Emmanuel Tsouderos, then Prime Minister and Minister of Foreign Affairs for Greece's exiled government; Lord Killearn, British Ambassador to Egypt; H. M. King Peter of Yugoslavia (I asked Father what he thought of Peter, who had apparently asked for direct American support to regain his slipping throne; Father looked astonished that anybody would seriously be interested in his opinion. "What would anyone think? He's just a boy. Any ideas he has somebody has thought up for him."); Pouritch, then Yugoslavia's Prime Minister and Minister for Foreign Affairs; Prince Paul of Greece; General Sir Henry Maitland Wilson, Commander-in-Chief of British Forces in the Middle East, together with General Royce, his American opposite; Air Chief Marshal Sir Sholto Douglas, commanding the RAF in the Middle East; Admiral Sir Algernon Willis, the British naval commander in the Levant; and General R. G. W. Stone, commanding British troops in Egypt.

At one point, while the traffic was lighter than usual, I snatched an opportunity to have a word with Harry Hopkins.

"I take it Father and the P.M. are having their fusses again," I said.

Harry shrugged. "With a difference, this time," he said. "In fact, with two differences. First place, we're turning out the stuff now. Tanks. Ships. Guns. That makes a difference. The war from now on will be fought with equipment made in America, and by men born in America, predominantly. Is that a difference?"

"Sure is."

"Who's senior partner, and who's junior?" He looked at me thoughtfully for a few seconds. "And yet, at the same time, Winston knows this conference is taking place on Empire soil. That makes a subtle difference. And another thing: this conference has an agenda unlike any of the others. This one is chiefly concerned with Far Eastern and Middle Eastern affairs—men and issues that are comparatively new to Americans, and to your father as well. Churchill and Eden—they've been steeped in Far Eastern and Middle Eastern affairs ever since they were in primary school. It's old stuff to them—it's the core of their Empire."

"Now who's senior partner and who's junior?" I put in.

"Don't worry about that," Harry assured me. "Your father still is. But he's taking his time, a little bit. He's still keeping his ears and his pores open. He's learning. But he's still boss."

I knocked off from my duties as greeter around four-thirty and went into a new act: sitting in for Father at the Chiangs' cocktail party. I found, when I got to their villa, one or two miles away, that Churchill's daughter

Sarah was performing a similar duty for *her* father. But I hadn't much opportunity to talk with her; Madame Chiang was at my side and leading me to two chairs almost at once. She struck me as quite a performer. For more than thirty minutes she talked animatedly, interestedly, intensely—and she always contrived to keep *me* the center of our conversation. It was as expert a job of flattery and charm as anybody had troubled to exert on me in years. She talked of her country, but only within the context of urging me to come out to China and settle there, after the war. I was interested in ranching? Then Northwest China was the place for me. As she painted a golden picture of the wealth an able and determined man could amass for himself, out of the toil of the Chinese coolies, she leaned forward, looking at me brightly, agreeing with everything I said, resting her hand firmly on my knee. For the first few minutes I insisted to myself that this lady was quite purely and simply interested in our conversation, and had no further motivation on her mind. But there was a hard brightness in her manner that was not compatible with complete sincerity. I do not for a second believe that she thought that I was so important that she must win me over, make me her fast friend, for any ulterior future purposes. What I do believe is that Madame Chiang has for so long a time dealt with people—and especially men—on the basis of winning charm and a simulated interest in those to whom she is talking that by now it is her second nature. And I would fear to watch her first nature at work; frankly, it would terrify me.

When she left me to go on to another guest, I got self a long stiff drink, and then wandered around, talking with people I knew. The room was full of brass and braid: everybody from all three Allied missions below the extreme top echelon was present; the air clattered with talk. I found a chance to be introduced to the Generalissimo, who speaks no English; we exchanged three or four aimless pleasantries through an interpreter. After an hour or so I made my goodbyes, and hurried back to Father's villa. He was still talking to Steinhardt when I got there; with them was George Allen, one of the State Department's experts on the Near East. I joined them as they were breaking up.

"How was the party?" he asked.

"Okay," I said. Steinhardt and Allen remained for a few moments, arranging when they should see Father again, after he had returned to Cairo from Teheran, discussing the advisability of their bringing Ismet Inonu, Turkish President, down to Cairo for an appointment, in view of Father's attitude toward Turkey's coming into the war. When they had left:

"I take it they agree with you that Turkey shouldn't come in," I said.

He nodded assent, and then returned to the subject of the cocktail party. He wanted to know how I had reacted to the Chiangs, and I told him especially what I had thought about Madame Chiang. Frowning thoughtfully, he listened until I finished, and then commented:

"I don't know that I'd put it as strongly as you do. She's an opportunist, certainly. And I'd certainly not want to be known as her enemy, in her own country. But at the moment, who is there in China who could take Chiang's place? There's just no other leader. With all their shortcomings, we've got to depend on the Chiangs."

I told him that while I was at the cocktail party, I had run into General Royce, and that he had invited me for dinner, and for an evening in Cairo afterwards. I asked permission to go, and he gave it.

"There's nothing special on for this evening, anyway. Just Harry and Bill Leahy, Pa Watson and Mac. Somebody said something about playing cards. You run along. Have fun."

So that night I went to a Cairo night club, with General Royce and some others; when I got back to Father's villa a little after midnight his guests were just leaving, and he and I went to his bedroom together. He wanted to know how my evening had gone, and I wanted to know if he had heard how the day's discussions among the Combined Chiefs had gone. Whenever I had passed the Mena House, I had seen officers, out on their balconies, sunning themselves and apparently continuing their talks while contriving at the same time to get a little fresh air and suntan.

Father said that his reports from Leahy indicated that there was progress, but still no final agreement. Still, and with considerable determination (which Father believed had its source in the Prime Minister), the British were pointing to the various real or imagined weaknesses in the plan for OVERLORD which had been drawn up in the summer and revised in the fall. Still, and with even more determination (which I could guess had *its* source in Father and General Marshall), the Americans were insisting on the wisdom of the operation, and fighting off slighter alternatives in Norway or the Mediterranean.

"I gather," Father commented, "that Marshall and King are discouraged to find that a plan, twice agreed on already, has to be fought out all over again. And I must say, I can understand their discouragement."

Apparently the frictions between British and American commanders in the CBI had contributed to some of the stiffness with which the British were resisting the planned operation in the west. The divergence here was quite simply that the British put no stock whatever in the concept that Chinese could be whipped together into any kind of fighting machine, in contradistinction to Stilwell's still unproven efforts; and that the British strategy in Burma was one of go slow and go small, as against our strategy of go as fast and as big as we could. I offered the comment that at least their military ideas made sense, taken in conjunction with their Empire commitments.

"Of course they do," said Father, explosively. "But their Empire ideas are nineteenth century, if not eighteenth or seventeenth. And we're fighting a twentieth-century war. Thanks be to God, the balance has shifted somewhat; it's no longer quite a war for survival; but it was a close thing, a very, very close thing; and one of the principal reasons it was a close thing lies in their assumption of the eternity of Empire.

"I give Winston the example of our approach to the

Philippines—the first steps of education we have insisted on, the efforts we have made to shift responsibility for the Philippines off our own shoulders and on to theirs . . ."

"What's his answer?"

"What do you think? He says the Filipinos are a different breed of people, naturally more self-reliant, naturally ready to take greater responsibility. He says we just don't understand the Indians, or the Burmese, or the Javanese, or . . . or even the Chinese!"

Father was relaxed, the day ahead of him was not a terribly busy one, he was inclined to talk further. We each lighted another cigarette, and chatted idly for a time of nothing in particular. We speculated about Teheran, what it would bring, what Uncle Joe would be like (he always referred to Stalin, when we were alone, as Uncle Joe).

"One thing I'm sure of," he chuckled, "and that is that I'll find an ally on the need for attacking Europe from the west. At that, by next spring, the way things are going in Russia now, maybe a second front won't be necessary!" At that time the Red Army was racing across the plains, closer and closer to the old Polish frontier, a hundred, then sixty, now only about fifty miles away. Kiev had been freed. We were both feeling pretty good: war's end by then really coming in sight; at that point I could remind Father, as I did, of his prediction that Germany would fall within another twelve months, without feeling that I might be putting a hex on our chances.

"Give me thirteen months, not just twelve, Elliott," he said. And then, "Say, I'd better make that fourteen, not thirteen, at that."

"At some point it'll have to be thirteen."

"No. It'll go from fourteen months away to twelve months, just as it does in Mother's apartment building, on Washington Square, remember? They skip the thirteenth floor."

"Say, it's after midnight, isn't it? It's really Thursday. I can wish you a good Thanksgiving Day."

"That's right. And with plenty to be thankful for, too."

Around one-thirty, I left him with a detective story, and went to bed.

The morning brought Averell Harriman and Sir Alexander Cadogan, then it brought an hour's work on mail that had arrived from Washington in the diplomatic pouch. Around noon the P.M. and the Chiangs came by, together with the members of their military and naval staffs, and everybody went out to the garden, to sit for pictures. At lunchtime the subject was supply again, with Lord Leathers and Ambassador Winant trading ideas with Lewis Douglas and John McCloy, Assistant Secretary of War. Just as we left the table, I was told that Major Otis Bryan had arrived; he and Mike Reilly had flown up to Teheran and back at our request, to see if the mountains were really high enough to justify Admiral McIntire's fears. When he saw me, Otis held up a thumb and forefinger, joined to make an emphatically approving circle. "It's okay," he reported. "If the weather isn't soup, we can make it easily, without ever going much over seven thousand."

Father was immensely cheered by the news; he had

not looked forward to the slow, hot train trip for a minute.

A big Thanksgiving banquet was in preparation all afternoon, back in the villa's ample kitchen, but the Chiangs were not going to be able to share it with us. Instead, the Generalissimo and his wife stopped in for tea; we were just four, sitting in the shade, out in the garden. Mostly Madame Chiang talked; persuasively she outlined her plans for increasing literacy in post-war China, on the basis of a sort of "Basic Chinese" which would cut the number of ideographs down to about as many words as are used in "Basic English"—some twelve or fifteen hundred. She talked, too, of other improvements planned for the future, and Father, who had always had great respect for the Chinese people, great interest in their problems and in the possibilities for developing their potentialities, listened with keen attention. Mindful of what he had said about the present unavailability of any other leader who could keep China in the war, I found myself wondering if he was not perhaps himself reflecting that these reforms which Madame Chiang was describing would not have to wait on some other force than the Chiangs.

Before they left, Madame Chiang, translating for her husband, made reference to a tentative agreement he had reached with Father toward furthering internal Chinese unity, specifically as regarded the Chinese Communists. I pricked up my ears, but the point was dropped almost at once; obviously it was a subject which had already been discussed in some detail. Chiang and Father, in any event, seemed perfectly in accord on the approach toward such unity.

The Thanksgiving dinner could not have been more pleasant. In the first place, it came at an auspicious moment. As Father and I had remarked the night before, the Soviet armies were sweeping all before them; another in the series of Allied conferences was drawing to what everyone hoped would be a successful close; another—perhaps the most eventful and important of all—was at hand; Allied unity, despite the stresses which were constantly placed upon it, seemed at its height, and was about to be extended in person to the Fourth of the Big Four; Tarawa and Makin, with their terrible cost, were behind us, as were the Gilberts; over Europe our air armadas were daily growing in might, as Berlin, after its fifth saturation raid, was rapidly discovering.

And so, as we sat down around the great long table in the Kirk villa that Thanksgiving night, we were in a mood to celebrate. Father had brought his own turkeys from home—they were gifts to him from Edward Stettinius, then Under Secretary of State, and from one Joe Carter, of Burnt Corn, Alabama. "Can you imagine how surprised Joe'll be, when he finds out how far his birds were flown, before they were eaten?" asked Father, as he carved one. And he carved, as he loved to do, for the whole company: Churchill, his daughter Sarah, Eden, Commander Thompson, Lord Moran, Leahy, Winant, Harriman, Hopkins and his son Bob, Pa Watson, Admirals McIntire and Brown, Steinhardt, Kirk himself, whose guests we all were, John Boettiger, and me. Outside, while we ate, an orchestra from Camp Huckstep, our military camp near Cairo, played dance music.

And toward the end, Father lifted a glass of wine to propose a toast. Briefly he touched on the custom of Thanksgiving, and how it had first come about; warmly he described how tonight, all over the world, American soldiers and sailors were bringing this American tradition to a score and more foreign lands. And then he said:

"And of course this leads me to the thought that I, personally, am delighted to be sharing this Thanksgiving dinner with Great Britain's Prime Minister."

Churchill was on his feet to respond to the toast, but Father was not yet finished.

"Large families," said Father, "are usually more closely united than small ones . . . and so, this year, with the peoples of the United Kingdom in our family, we are a large family, and more united than ever before. I propose a toast to this unity, and may it long continue!"

The P.M. answered the toast; it is a remarkable thing, his ability for impromptu oratory. In his response he, too, praised our wartime unity and pledged its continued strength.

The only time that Father had been able to arrange for his private talk with General Stilwell was after dinner that night. The tall, wiry soldier arrived around ten, and by ten-thirty he and Father were sitting beside each other on the couch in the living room, their heads together. I was sitting some feet away with my brother-in-law John and Harry Hopkins—the three of us talked every now and then, but more often we listened.

"Vinegar Joe" Stilwell talked easily, forthrightly, and quietly. He never raised his voice, and rarely offered any complaints, although it was not difficult to imagine that he would have been justified in doing either or both. A tough row to hoe, that was his lot. He described his difficulties with Chiang and General Ho, Chiang's War Minister; then, in answer to a question from Father, he laconically ventured his judgment that he would be able to handle such difficulties. He mentioned that his task would be easier, were he in the position to offer more Lend-Lease, and in the same breath anticipated Father's reasons for finding it next to impossible to raise the quotas. Father asked about the Ledo Road; he wanted first-hand information on the problems posed and the possibilities of success at that fifth-magnitude engineering job. The British, Father had learned, were citing everything from malaria to weather as reasons for not undertaking the road. But by this time, in the Mena House conferences, American thinking had carried the day, and Stilwell argued quietly and convincingly the case for the road with Father. At Cairo, an effort had been made by the British to revise some of the tonnage quotas for supplies to the CBI agreed upon at Quebec, not so much revisions downward as revisions in the direction those supplies should take, and Stilwell touched on his disagreement with those revisions, urging that any change in the Quebec quotas should be upward.

Stilwell had no need to debate with Father the possibilities of the Chinese as fighters; on this point Father was readily prepared to be the General's advocate. But Father was interested in what progress Stilwell's training had accomplished, and he was told that at that moment two divisions of American-trained Chinese troops were in the field. "Not yet fighting as well as they might," Stilwell admitted, somewhat wrily. "As a matter of fact, I'm anxious to get right back there—help them over their first frights. Stage frights, no more, I'm sure, although unfortunately the British learned about their first performance under fire, and promptly made a great point of it." But he was sure that his estimate of Chinese fighting ability would eventually be proven; and, as always with such a fine general, it is a pleasure to know, today, that he was right.

It was clear that Father liked General Stilwell: he kept him beside him on the couch for nearly an hour; only then, and with an expression of sympathy from Father on the thorny path he had before him in the East, did he take his leave.

And later, when I was once more smoking a goodnight cigarette with Father in his bedroom, he talked some more about that thorny path. He began by telling me that the British were set even against the strategy we were pursuing in the Pacific theater.

"They don't approve of our island-hopping," he said. "And they don't begin to understand our thinking in terms of the Philippines, as a future base for operations against Japan." He smiled, a little sourly. "Perhaps they don't appreciate the fact that the Filipinos will rally to our flag, inasmuch as they could hardly expect *their* colonials to rally to *theirs*.

"Anyway," he went on, "their idea is that we should forget about the island-hopping and concentrate on clearing the Malay Peninsula, after which we'd be able to crawl on up the Chinese coast, and make a base for the future against Japan there."

I had heard some scuttlebutt from our own Navy's officers about landings on the coast of China.

"Oh, certainly," said Father. "That's quite in the cards. But much farther north than the British think will ever prove feasible. Once again, our intelligence gives us a different picture from that of the British. They see only a Chinese coast infested with Japanese, while we are fully aware of the fact that much of that coast is in the hands of Chinese guerrillas."

I asked if these guerrillas were the Chinese Communist troops, and he nodded an affirmative.

"Incidentally," he said, "Chiang would have us believe that the Chinese Communists are doing nothing against the Japanese. Again, we know differently."

Independently, I had come by the information that all our photographic air reconnaissance and aerial mapping of Chinese terrain, photographs which our Fourteenth Air Force of course had to have, was strictly withheld from British view, and I mentioned that fact to Father. He knew about it, too.

"We worked out that arrangement with the Chinese quite some time ago," he said. "The Chinese were very anxious that we agree not to show our air-maps to the British—in fact, they made us promise not to before we went ahead with the work. It's not hard to appreciate their point of view. They're aware that the British want a look at them for commercial reasons . . . commercial, postwar reasons.

"Matter of fact, I was talking to Chiang about that at dinner, a few days ago. You see, he wants very badly to get our support against the British moving into Hong Kong and Shanghai and Canton with the same old extra-territorial rights they enjoyed before the war."

I asked if we were going to give such support.

"Not for nothing," Father answered. "Before it came up, I'd been registering a complaint about the character of Chiang's government. I'd told him it was hardly the modern democracy that ideally it should be. I'd told him he would have to form a unity government, *while the war was still being fought*, with the Communists in Yenan. And he agreed. He agreed, contingently. He agreed to the formation of a democratic government once he had our assurance that the Soviet Union would agree to respect the frontier in Manchuria. That part of it is on the agenda for Teheran."

"So then, if you're able to work out that end of it with Stalin, Chiang has agreed to form a more democratic government in China. And in return . . ."

"In return, we will support his contention that the British and other nations no longer enjoy special Empire rights to Hong Kong, Shanghai, and Canton. That's right."

It was quite a deal, and promised good things.

"I was especially happy to hear the Generalissimo agree to invite the Communists in as part of the National Government *prior* to elections," Father said. "Actually, as far as he's concerned, the only earnest of our good faith that he expects is that when Japan is on her knees we make sure that no British warships come into Chinese ports. Only American warships. And I've given him my personal promise that that's what will happen."

"Tough to get agreement from Churchill on any part of that one," I observed.

"There can't be much argument, inasmuch as it's ninety-nine per cent American matériel and American men bringing about the defeat of Japan," Father said, sharply. "American foreign policy after the war must be along the lines of bringing about a realization on the part of the British and the French and the Dutch that the way we have run the Philippines is the only way they can run *their* colonies." And he went on to point out that a majority of Chinese think more highly of Japanese colonial policies than they do of British or French or Dutch.

Father had discussed more than just China's future with the Generalissimo. They had talked together about the Malay States, about Burma and Indo-China and India. And, obviously, Chiang had been cheered by Father's attitude on these colonial questions. For Father had said that, whereas in India the British should be made content to maintain economic preferential treatment while granting political independence, the French would have no right, after the war, simply to walk back into Indo-China and reclaim that rich land for no reason other than it had once been their colony. And he had insisted to Chiang that the most the French should have was a trusteeship of their colonies responsible to a United Nations organization, looking toward eventual independence, once the United Nations were satisfied that the colonies could manage their own affairs. It was the same opinion he had expressed nearly a year before, and time had done nothing but strengthen his convictions.

Next day, after a morning full of appointments with James Landis and Averell Harriman and Lord Louis Mountbatten (who had his own side of the wrangling in the CBI to report to Father) and Madame Chiang and Admiral Leahy and Ambassador Winant, I finally got a moment alone with him to tell him that the Legion of Merit medal he had asked me to send for had arrived.

"Fine!" he cried. It was just the kind of surprise he loved to spring. "Make sure that Ike can step over here from the Mena House after lunch."

And so, around two-thirty, when General Eisenhower came with General Marshall, Father announced that he had a little surprise in store. General Ike stood ramrod straight when Father asked Pa Watson to read the citation that had been prepared. Father motioned, when the citation had been read, for Ike to step forward and, as the General leaned down, Father pinned the medal on his tunic.

"You deserve this, and much more, Ike," said Father.

And Ike, his eyes filled with tears, said, "It's the happiest moment of my life, sir. I appreciate this decoration more than any other you could give me."

The afternoon was given over to a final political conference. The Chiangs, the Prime Minister, Harriman, Eden, and Cadogan were with the President in the garden for some two hours, framing the language of the communiqué which would be released following the

Teheran Conference, deciding on the words from which the world would learn that Manchuria, Formosa, and the Pescadores would revert to China, and that Korea would once more after many years be free.

A quiet dinner, and an early bedtime, for Father and his party had to be up by five next morning, if they were to reach Teheran in the afternoon. The weather had been reported fair; plans for flight the whole distance held good. I was not going with his party; Major Leon Gray had flown to Cairo with my plane, which I proposed to use to get to Teheran, for it was not certain how long I would be able to stay in Iran, and I had to have a way to get back at a moment's notice. And besides, I had been invited by General Eisenhower to take in some sightseeing farther south, at Luxor, for a day.

So next afternoon, after Father's party had left, Leon Gray and I, together with a member of our crew, Sergeant Cram, headed down the Nile to join Ike and some of his staff. We got there Saturday night, and found our rooms in the Luxor Hotel. It was not all we found in that hotel either: in a room just off the lobby there was a battered old upright piano, and with a crow of pleasure Sgt. Cram went right for it. He had been, in more peaceful days, pianist with Kay Kyser's band, and with real joy he settled down, flexed his fingers, and went to work. For over two hours, after dinner, he played for us and for Ike, and we just sat back and listened. If you shut your eyes, you were home again, and the war was over.

Next day, the tombs of the Pharaohs, a picnic lunch in some old beat-up Fords, a trip through the great majestic temple at Karnak—a day of peace and rest and leisure. The only concern exhibited by any of our party was General Eisenhower's nagging worry that out of the conferences at Cairo and Teheran, out of the final discussions on the invasion of Europe from the west, would come the decision that General Marshall would be in command of that last Allied push, while he, Eisenhower, would be kicked upstairs into a desk job in the Pentagon. Three or four times during the course of the afternoon he plaintively voiced his concern; I was never quite sure whether or not he was doing it just because a son of the Commander-in-Chief was in the near vicinity: at any rate, there was nothing I could have done, even if I had felt that it was any of my business to try. All I could say was something to the effect that: "The Joint Chiefs will surely consult you, sir, before they take any final action." And even of that I was by no means sure.

Leon Gray, Sgt. Cram, and I had planned to take off for Teheran the next day, but our B-25 was acting up strangely, so we had to spend some time getting it smooth again. We finally took off, the late afternoon of Monday the 29th, planning to fly over the deserts of Arabia, with one refueling stop at Habanayah at four in the morning.

Nine-thirty Tuesday morning we settled down at the airport in Teheran, only to find that we had been the unwitting cause of a lot of fuss and feathers. Communications being what they were in that part of the world, we had been unable to let Father know we were a day delayed in Luxor, with the consequence that everyone was sure we had been forced down somewhere in the Arabian desert. They were just about to order the search planes out. Indeed, it would have been no pleasure if we had been forced down, for as everybody knew only too well, the nomads of Saudi Arabia are rough and tough characters. So Father was a mite relieved. As a matter of fact, so was I.

7

TEHERAN CONFERENCE

THE SEVENTY-SEVEN Americans who made up the party to Teheran saw it first from the air—a surprisingly modern city, its buildings and railroad yards clustered at the foot of a range of small mountains. These mountains, taken with others to the west and south, formed a bowl which enclosed miles and miles of desert, an occasional village, one or two lonesome spurs of railroad track, and Teheran. The Big Three were met here in compromise, and I imagine none of the three chief participants was completely happy about the place of rendezvous. Stalin, because he was a working military commander, had insisted that it be some city no farther than a day's flight from Moscow; and as a result here they were, in the capital of a friendly neutral, a country which was one of the United Nations, but of which it was difficult to make any other recommendation.

But it was never difficult to hit on a drawback. For one: until quite recently, Teheran had been general headquarters for all Axis espionage in the Middle East;

and Mike Reilly of our Secret Service shared with the Soviet secret service agents the conviction that there were still, despite many precautions, among the thousands of refugees who had crowded into the city from Europe, dozens of Nazi agents and sympathizers. For another: the problems of health and sanitation are among the most difficult in the world. Teheran's drinking water flows down to the city from the mountains in open ditches; if you live on the upper outskirts of the city, you are fortunate, for you have first crack at it; you are probably also antisocial, for you use the ditches as they flow past you as sewage system as well as water supply system; thus, if you are unfortunate enough to live in the center or lower outskirts of the city, what you get as drinking water is your neighbor's refuse and offal. After that, you are surprised if you don't get typhus or malaria or dysentery. Why a city with broad, well-paved streets, relatively modern hospitals, a university, museums, a serviceable power plant—even a telephone system—should not have taken the seemingly prior step of installing a proper water supply system and sewage disposal system is one of those minor mysteries.

And despite the fact that Teheran otherwise gave the appearance of a modern and prosperous city, it was swiftly evident that the Iranian economy was neither modern nor prosperous. There was the capital, and then there was the surrounding country—a grazing ground for the herds of nomadic tribes, who knew nothing but abject poverty except perhaps in the north, where there was better farmland and a better living to be won. To the south were the oil fields, then a British concession, which had brought great wealth to a thin stratum of upper-class Persians and Government officials, but had brought precisely nothing to any other citizen.

As if all this were not bad enough, the war had brought in its train a flourishing inflation: a sack of flour cost more than a whole year's income of the Iranian who was not a Government official in Teheran; refugees had to pay the equivalent of five dollars for a pack of American cigarettes, two thousand American dollars for an automobile tire, eight thousand dollars for a radio, fifteen hundred for a Swiss wrist-watch.

In the face of this onslaught on the cost of living, the Iranian officials had thrown up their hands, but had done nothing else.

All these things, of course, we found out only after we had been a few days in the capital. The first morning of our arrival, we spent an hour trying to get an Army car to come down to the field and pick us up, and idly examining the field itself—with rows of Lend-Lease P-39's, complete with their freshly painted red stars—after which I spent another hour driving through Teheran to the wrong addresses. The first place I headed for, of course, was the American Legation, but there I was told Father was in residence at the Soviet Embassy. There were, I learned, good reasons for this. At first Father had declined the invitation—which had been extended by Marshal Stalin himself—on the grounds that he would be more independent if he were no one's guest, and that he had also declined a prior British invitation and hesitated to run the possibility of offending them by then accepting the Russian offer. But convenience and, even more important, security, dictated ultimate acceptance. The American Legation was considerably removed from both the British Embassy and the Soviet Embassy; the latter two were separated from each other only by a city street. And infested as the city undoubtedly was by Axis spies—Soviet secret service agents were to announce later that they had arrested men plotting specifically against the lives of the Big Three—it was the dictate of good sense to live in the safest possible place. Ambassador Harriman took pains to point out to Father that if anything were to happen either to British or to Soviet officials on their way to the American Legation Father would himself feel responsible.

Certainly the Russians did everything possible to make Father's stay in their Embassy pleasant: Stalin himself retired to one of the smaller houses within the compound, leaving Father the main building; and the excellent USN Filipino cooks and stewards came along, too, to prepare meals as they had at Cairo. Further, there was real convenience for Father in the arrangement, for his suite opened right into the board room of the Embassy in which all the plenary meetings of the conference were to be held.

In any event, it was not until after eleven that Monday morning that I finally saw Father—and discovered for the first time that he had been worried over my lateness.

"Haven't you got enough on your mind, Pop, what with meeting Stalin and all, without worrying about whether my plane is late or not?"

"What was the matter? We called down to Palestine . . ."

Palestine had first been suggested by Eisenhower for our two-day sightseeing trip; only after Father had left did Ike decide to go down to Luxor instead.

"I'm sorry, Pop. If we'd been able to radio you . . ."

"And especially after the British told us what happened to men who are forced to crash-land in Arabia," he said.

I asked him if he were busy, if I should beat it and come back later.

"Nothing except some mail from Washington," he said. "Sit down and visit for a few minutes."

We were in the sitting room of his suite, a plain, comfortable, solidly furnished room on the ground floor. It looked out on the compound, alive with cheerful gardens. I sat down on the couch with him. I was tired from the long night's flight, yet I was excited, too, and curious: the meeting Father had been working to set up for more than a year, for more than twelve bloody, desperate months, had now come to pass.

"What's he like, Pop? Or haven't you seen him yet?"

"Uncle Joe? Sure. Sure, I've seen him. I wanted to have him over for dinner, Saturday night, but he sent back word he was too tired. When I came over here yesterday he came up to say hello. Yesterday afternoon, it was."

"Right here?"

He laughed at me. "Right on this couch, Elliott. The Marshal sat right where you're sitting."

"What about the P.M.?"

"This first time, it was just me and Uncle Joe. And his interpreter, of course, Pavlov."

I asked him if Charles Bohlen, the State Department expert on Russian affairs, had not been present as well.

"Well," Father smiled, "it was suggested to me. But the way I looked at it, it would be taken as a gesture of my confidence and my lack of suspicion if *his* interpreter were the only one present. And—as a matter of fact—it simplifies matters a whole lot, too. Saves time."

I nodded agreement. It *was* a good idea—even if Stalin were completely without suspicion of the Anglo-Americans. It was bound to put everything on an informal, non-protocol basis of friendship and warm alliance.

"What'd you talk about?" I asked. "Or was it state secrets?"

"Not a bit of it," Father said. "Mostly, it was 'How did I like my quarters?' and 'Thank you very much for turning over the main house to me' and 'What is the news from the eastern front?' (It's very good, by the way; Stalin's most pleased; he hopes the Red Army will have crossed the Polish border before we leave.) That sort of thing. Polite chit-chat. I didn't specially want to start in on business right straight off the bat."

"Measuring each other, eh?"

He frowned. "I wouldn't say that."

"I was kidding."

"We were getting to know each other. We were finding out what kind of people we are."

"What kind of people is he?"

"Oh . . . he's got a kind of massive rumble, talks deliberately, seems very confident, very sure of himself, moves slowly—altogether quite impressive, I'd say."

"You like him?"

He nodded an emphatic affirmative. Stalin had stayed only a few minutes, then Foreign Commissar Molotov had come by, for *his* official call, and at four the Big Three had held their first plenary meeting. Once again the British had had the greatest number of delegates—eight, headed of course by Churchill; we Americans had had seven representatives—Father, Hopkins, Leahy, King, Major General Deane (who was our military attaché at Moscow), Captain Royal, and Bohlen; and it was the Russians who were in the minority—just Stalin, Molotov, Voroshilov, a secretary, and Pavlov, Stalin's interpreter.

"And," Father grinned, "Stalin was shown a copy of our plan for OVERLORD. He looked at it, asked a question or two, and then just asked: 'When?' "

I commented that it must have been quite a meeting, and asked where Marshall and Arnold had been, during all this. It turned out they had got their signals mixed and were on an automobile ride through Teheran.

"I'm sure we'll hit it off, Stalin and I," Father said. "A great deal of the misunderstandings and the mistrusts of the past are going to get cleared up during the next few days—I hope once and for all. As for Uncle Joe and Winston, well . . ."

"Not so good, eh?"

"I'll have my work cut out for me, in between those two. They're *so* different. Ideas, temperaments . . ."

Father told me of the dinner he had given the night before, for Stalin and Churchill and the top diplomatic advisers, and of how after dinner they had sat around until eleven o'clock, talking politics slowly, feeling their way, the need for interpretation a small barrier, the diametrically opposed views of Stalin and Churchill a great barrier. He was amused by one quite human reaction of the P.M.'s to Marshal Stalin—although at Casablanca Churchill had dressed usually in pin-stripe blue, and in Cairo generally in summer whites, now at Teheran, faced with the Marshal's uniform, he had taken to wearing one of his own: that of a high-ranking RAF officer.

I was curious to know what sort of politics had been discussed.

"About everything we could think of," Father said. He mentioned the peace of the postwar world, the structure of the three nations that would hold the peace, the fact that there was explicit agreement that any peace would have to depend on these three nations acting in united fashion, to the point where—on an important question—negative action by only one of them would veto the entire proposition. Father said that this question of a single veto had yet to be discussed thoroughly, but indicated that he was, generally speaking, in favor of the principle, in view of the hard-rock necessity of the future and continuing unity of the Three. "And we agreed that the peace will be kept by force, if necessary," he added. "Our principal job was to come to agreement as to what constitutes the area of general security, in the postwar world, for each of our countries. That job is still before us, but we've made a start on it."

Father's secretary, Lieutenant Rigdon, stuck his head in to remind Father there was that mail from Washington to be cleared up, and I started to leave. Father called me back.

"By the way," he said, a triumphant look in his eye, "I don't suppose you've heard yet about the game on Saturday."

"The game?" I asked, blankly.

"Army-Navy. You *would* join the Army, would you? That'll be ten dollars, please. Thirteen to nothing." And he held out his hand.

"I wish you'd keep your mind on affairs of state," I complained, paying up.

Across the hall, in the Embassy's board room, I could hear voices: American, British, and Soviet staff members were inside, hard at it. I made my way outside, to the compound, to have a look around. The place was filled with Russian guardsmen, most of them officers, and all of them really big men. Nothing under six feet two. I strolled around long enough to discover that with screens and guards the Soviet Embassy and the British Embassy had been in effect combined into one large compound, surrounded entirely by watchful men, many of them, I assumed from their civilian dress, Soviet secret service agents. On each there was a suspicious bulge; they appeared to be loaded with fairly heavy artillery; Stalin seemed to be taking no chances on the security of his guests.

After lunch, Father met with the American chiefs of staff to hear what progress had been made that morning. They were short and snappy: in a fast fifteen minutes

Leahy, Marshall, and the others told of the conversations, chiefly concerned with Overlord, its time, its weight, its command.

And when they had left to resume their talks with their British opposites and the slender Soviet staff, I joined Father, in some excitement, to be with him when Stalin and Molotov came by appointment. Punctual to the minute, the Soviet leaders arrived with slender Pavlov. I was introduced. We pulled up chairs in front of Father's couch, and I sat back to collect my thoughts.

In spite of the fact that I had been told Stalin was shorter than average, I was surprised. I was also feeling pretty good, for I had received a very friendly greeting, together with a twinkle in the eye which invited me to smile. As he spoke—first offering Father and me each a Russian cigarette, two or three puffs of strong, black tobacco at the end of a two-inch cardboard holder—I realized something else about him: that his quiet, deep, measured voice and his short stature notwithstanding, he had a tremendously dynamic quality; inside him there seemed to be great reserves of patience and of assurance. Beside him, his Foreign Commissar, Molotov, was gray and colorless, a sort of carbon copy of my Uncle Theodore Roosevelt as I remember him. Listening to Stalin's quiet words, watching his quick, flashing smile, I sensed the determination that is in his name: Steel.

In the forty-five minutes that followed, Father and he did most of the talking. At first I paid most attention to our visitor—noting his beige uniform, well made and well cut. But after a time I listened to their words: they were discussing the Far East, China, the things that Father had already discussed with Generalissimo Chiang. Father was explaining Chiang's anxiety to end Britain's extraterritorial rights in Shanghai and Hong Kong and Canton, his anxiety about Manchuria, and the need for the Soviets' respecting the Manchurian frontier. Stalin made the point that world recognition of the sovereignty of the Soviet Union was a cardinal principle with him, that most certainly he would respect, in turn, the sovereignty of other countries, large or small. Father went on to the other aspects of his conversation with Chiang, the promise that the Chinese Communists would be taken into the Government *before* any national Chinese elections, that these elections would take place as soon as possible after the war had been won. Stalin punctuated his remarks, as they were translated, with nods: he seemed in complete agreement.

This was the only phase of policy that the two discussed during this interview. For the rest, it was completely informal and relaxed, until, when it was nearly half-past three, Pa Watson looked in the door and announced that everything was ready. We got up and moved into the board room.

What things were ready for was a formal presentation ceremony: Churchill was to give Stalin, on behalf of his King and the British people, a mighty two-handed sword, tribute to the heroes and heroines of indomitable Stalingrad, where the back of the Nazi offensive had been forever broken, and the myth of Nazi invincibility forever dissolved.

The board room was filled with men: an honor guard of Red Army officers and British Tommies, a Red Army band, and the military and naval leaders of the three great powers combined against the Nazis. When Father and I entered, Stalin and Churchill were already present; the Red Army band was playing first the Soviet, then the British National Anthem. The sound filled the room, and poured out of the open windows; and each man's face was solemn. The Prime Minister said:

"I have been commanded by His Majesty King George VI to present to you for transmission to the City of Stalingrad this sword of honor, the design of which His Majesty has chosen and approved. The sword of honor was made by English craftsmen whose ancestors have been employed in sword-making for generations. The blade of the sword bears the inscription: 'To the steel-hearted citizens of Stalingrad, a gift from King George VI as a token of the homage of the British people.'"

A British junior officer had handed Churchill the great sword. He took it, swung around, and passed it over to the Marshal. Behind him, the Red Army guard stood silent but not entirely expressionless. Their carbines angled across their chests, they watched as their commander took the sword from Churchill, held it briefly, and then raised it to his mouth, to kiss its hilt. He swallowed, hard. His answer was translated for us:

"On behalf of the citizens of Stalingrad, I wish to express my deep appreciation for the gift of King George VI. The citizens of Stalingrad will value this gift most highly, and I ask you, Mr. Prime Minister, to convey their thanks to His Majesty the King."

There was a pause, and then the Marshal gravely walked around the corner of the table to where Father was sitting, and offered the sword for inspection. The P.M. held the scabbard, while Father pulled out the fifty inches of tempered steel. Up it flashed, aloft, its blade glittering in my eyes where I stood, directly behind Father. His hands looked small on the sword's great hilt. Four hands could have fitted on that haft. From an Empire, a King had dispatched by his Tory Prime Minister a gift forged by craftsmen who, in their skill, were themselves aristocrats, working an aristocratic and medieval trade. Now the gift was given to the son of a shoe-cobbler, a Bolshevik, leader of a dictatorship of the proletariat, who watched impassively as the leader of the world's greatest arsenal of production held it straight up.

"Truly they had hearts of steel," murmured Father.

With a ring, the sword returned into its scabbard. The moment of their greatest unity over, the Prime Minister and the Marshal adjourned to the portico of the Embassy, where their pictures were to be taken with Father.

The three sat in chairs placed in the middle of the six great pillars of the portico. Around them were ranged their ministers, their ambassadors and generals and admirals. In front of them photographers knelt, crouched, leaned over motion-picture camera tripods, ran forward and backward for better perspective. The leading delegates gathered closer for a group picture, Sarah Churchill Oliver in her WAAF uniform among them. There was a pause while she was introduced to the Marshal, who rose punctiliously and bent over her hand. Fifteen swift minutes, and it was over. The arguments were to begin again.

This time there were twelve Americans and eleven Britons and five Russians. And they talked for more than three hours. Five o'clock, six, seven o'clock went by, while I waited in Father's apartment, and snatched a very welcome nap. At length, about a quarter after seven, Father woke me when he came in, and by this time he was pretty tired, too, and showed it.

"I'm going to have to get dressed for dinner," he complained. "I certainly would like to nap a little before."

"Why don't you?"

"Do you know, I think I'm too tired, and too on edge."

"Drink help?"

"Not right away, thanks. I'll wait and maybe have a cocktail before I start dressing. Right now I just want to lie down." He added, "Stalin is host tonight; that means a dinner Russian style; and if our State Department experts haven't erred again, that means plenty of toasts during dinner!"

He closed his eyes, but not to sleep; presently he rubbed them with both hands, pushing his glasses off; then he sighed and reached for one of my cigarettes.

"He gets things done, that man. He really keeps his eye on the ball he's aiming at." Father spoke slowly and thoughtfully. "It's a pleasure working with him. There's nothing devious. He outlines the subject he wants discussed, and he sticks to it."

"OVERLORD?"

"That's what *he* was talking about. And what *we* were talking about."

"British still raising objections, are they?"

"Well . . . now Winston is talking about two operations at once. I guess he knows there's no use trying to argue against the western invasion any more. Marshall has got to the point where he just looks at the P.M. as though he can't believe his ears." Father laughed, remembering. "If there's one American general that Winston can't abide, it's General Marshall. And needless to say, it's because Marshall's right. I hope, some day, everybody in America will realize what a debt he owes to George Marshall. There's just nobody like him. Nobody!"

"What does Churchill mean, Pop, two invasions at once?"

"One in the west, and one up through guess where."

"The Balkans?"

"Of course." Again he chuckled, as he thought back to the meeting. He leaned up on an elbow to look at me while he said, "You know, Elliott, it's an extraordinary thing, these plenary sessions, from one standpoint. Whenever the P.M. argued for our invasion through the Balkans, it was quite obvious to everyone in the room what he really meant. That he was above all else anxious to knife up into central Europe, in order to keep the Red Army out of Austria and Rumania, even Hungary, if possible. Stalin knew it, I knew it, everybody knew it. . . ."

"But he never said it?"

"Certainly not. And Uncle Joe, when he argued the military advantages of invasion from the west, and the inadvisability of splitting our forces into two parts—*he* was always conscious of the political implications, too,

I'm sure. Never let on, though, by so much as a word." He lay back again, silent.

"I don't suppose . . ." I began hesitantly.

"Hmmm?"

"What I mean is, Churchill . . . well, he isn't . . ."

"You wondering whether maybe he isn't right? That maybe it *would* be advisable for us to hit the Balkans, too?"

"Well . . ."

"Elliott: our chiefs of staff are convinced of one thing. The way to kill the most Germans, with the least loss of American soldiers, is to mount one great big invasion and then slam 'em with everything we've got. It makes sense to me. It makes sense to Uncle Joe. It makes sense to all our generals, and always has, ever since the beginning of the war and, I expect, since before that, too. Ever since our War Plans Division first started figuring out what we would do, when, as, and if. It makes sense to the Red Army people. That's that. It's the quickest way to win the war. That's all.

"Trouble is, the P.M. is thinking too much of the *post*-war, and where England will be. He's scared of letting the Russians get too strong.

"Maybe the Russians will get strong in Europe. Whether that's bad depends on a whole lot of factors.

"The one thing I'm sure of is this: if the way to save American lives, the way to win as short a war as possible, is from the west and from the west alone, without wasting landing-craft and men and matériel in the Balkan mountains, and our chiefs are convinced it is, then that's that!"

He smiled, but grimly. "I see no reason for putting the lives of American soldiers in jeopardy in order to protect real or fancied British interests on the European continent. We're at war, and our job is to win it as fast as possible, and without adventures. I think—I *hope*—that he's learned we mean that, once, finally, and for all." He closed his eyes again, and there was silence except for the ticking of a clock, which reminded me of the time.

"Run you a bath, Pop?"

"Time is it? Oh, my! Yes . . . and ask Arthur to come in, too, will you? And about that cocktail you were talking about a few minutes ago. . . ."

"Old-fashioned?"

"But a weak one, Elliott. Remember all those toasts coming up!"

The dinner that night took place in a dining room which opened off the board room. Marshal Stalin had invited, besides Father and the P.M., Anthony Eden, Molotov, Harriman, Harry Hopkins, Clark Kerr, and, as interpreters, Bohlen, Berezhkov, and Major Birse. I had not been invited, but during the first course one of the Russian secret service men standing in back of Stalin noticed me at a side entrance, and he leaned over and whispered to Stalin. I could see the Marshal look up and over in my direction, and I started to beat a hasty and embarrassed retreat; but he was on his feet at once, and came over to fetch me. With gestures, he made it quite clear that he wanted me to join the party; an interpreter doubled his invitation in English, explaining that the Marshal said graciously that he had not realized his secretary had not invited me. Insistently he took me by the arm and pulled me back into the room, and a place was made for me between Eden and Harriman.

So there I was, at my first Russian-style banquet. And all the stories you may have heard about them are true.

Of course, vodka; and fortunately also a still white wine, light and dry, and a Russian champagne, to my taste very good. I say 'fortunately,' for there was no conversation without a drink; it would have been a contradiction in terms. The only way we talked was through the medium of proposing a toast. It may sound cumbersome, but if your staying power is good you find that it develops into quite a lot of fun. Thus, if you want to say something on even as vapid a subject as the weather, it becomes:

"I wish to propose a toast to the magnificent weather we have been enjoying!" And you are on your feet to do it, and everybody else rises to his feet, and you all drink. Quite a system. It can even be political:

"I wish to propose a toast," cried a Russian, "to your future deliveries of Lend-Lease matériel which I am sure will arrive on time in the future, and will not be arriving late, as have shipments to date!" Everyone rises, glasses are emptied, everyone sits down again. In a situation like this, vodka can be your worst friend, but I noticed that Stalin stuck to vodka all through the meal, his glass being refilled each time from his own private bottle next to him. It wasn't water, either; for once he filled my glass with it, coming around the table to do so. If it was anything less than one hundred proof, I most emphatically do not wish to be offered the real thing. By and large, I stuck to the champagne, feeling that American honor was at stake.

The courses followed each other in greatest profusion. I have a theory about the number of courses at a Russian dinner, too: the reason there are so many is that you don't have too much opportunity to get a bite of any one of them; you're on your feet too often, exchanging conversa . . . I mean, toasts. About halfway through dinner, Harry Hopkins, who had not been feeling any too well to begin with, excused himself. The first American defection. Grimly—and by now a little hilariously, too—the rest of us stayed by our glasses.

Toward the end of the meal Uncle Joe arose to propose his umpteenth toast—for a time I had been trying to keep count, but by then I was hopelessly lost—and it was on the subject of the Nazi war criminals. I cannot hope to remember his words exactly, but it ran something like this:

"I propose a salute to the swiftest possible justice for all Germany's war criminals—justice before a firing squad. I drink to our unity in dispatching them as fast as we capture them, all of them, and there must be at least fifty thousand of them."

Quick as a flash Churchill was on his feet. (By the way, the P.M. stuck to his favorite brandy throughout the toasting; his nightly regimen of cognac prepared him well for Russian-style conversation; but that night I suspect that even such a redoubtable tippler as he was finding his tongue thicker than usual.) His face and neck were red.

"Any such attitude," he cried, "is wholly contrary to

our British sense of justice! The British people will never stand for such mass murder. I take this opportunity to say that I feel most strongly that no one, Nazi or no, shall be summarily dealt with, before a firing squad, without proper legal trial, no matter what the known facts and proven evidence against him!"

I glanced at Stalin: he seemed hugely tickled, but his face remained serious; only his eyes twinkled as he took up the P.M.'s challenge and drew him on, suavely pricking his arguments, seemingly careless of the fact that Churchill's temper was now hopelessly lost. At length, Stalin turned to Father and asked *his* opinion. Father, who had been hiding a smile, nevertheless felt that the moment was beginning to be too highly charged with bad feeling: it was his notion to inject a witticism.

"As usual," he said, "it seems to be my function to mediate this dispute. Clearly there must be some sort of compromise between your position, Mr. Stalin, and that of my good friend the Prime Minister. Perhaps we could say that, instead of summarily executing fifty thousand war criminals, we should settle on a smaller number. Shall we say forty-nine thousand five hundred?"

Americans and Russians laughed. The British, taking their cue from their Prime Minister's mounting fury, sat quiet and straight-faced. Stalin, on top of the situation, pursued Father's compromise figure; he asked around the table for agreement of new estimates. The British were careful: The subject requires and deserves a great deal of study, they said. The Americans, on the other hand, were more jocular: Let's brush it off—we're still miles and miles and months and months away from Germany and conquest of the Nazis. I was hoping that Stalin would be satisfied by the early answers, and change the subject before he got to me, but if he is anything, he is persistent. The question came. Somewhat uncertainly I got to my feet.

"Well," I said, and took a deep breath, trying to think fast through the champagne bubbles. "Isn't the whole thing pretty academic? Look: when our armies start rolling in from the west, and your armies are still coming on from the east, we'll be solving the whole thing, won't we? Russian, American, and British soldiers will settle the issue for most of those fifty thousand, in battle, and I hope that not only those fifty thousand war criminals will be taken care of, but many hundreds of thousands more Nazis as well." And I started to sit down again.

But Stalin was beaming with pleasure. Around the table he came, flung an arm around my shoulders. An excellent answer! A toast to my health! I flushed with pleasure, and was about to drink, for it is the Russian custom for one to drink even when it is his own health that is proposed, when all of a sudden an angry finger was being waved right in my face.

"Are you interested in damaging relations between the Allies? Do you know what you are saying? How can you dare say such a thing?" It was Churchill—and he was furious, and no fooling. Somewhat shaken to find the Prime Minister and the Marshal squabbling right over my head and feeling a little like Alice-in-Wonderland being crowded by the Hatter and the March Hare at the celebrated Tea Party, I regained my chair, and sat quiet, worried stiff.

Fortunately the dinner broke up soon afterward, and I followed Father back to his apartment to apologize. After all, damaging relations between the Allies!

Father roared with laughter. "Don't think a second about it," he insisted. "What you said was perfectly all right. It was fine. Winston just lost his head when everybody refused to take the subject seriously. Uncle Joe . . . the way he was needling him, he was going to take offense at what anybody said, specially if what was said pleased Uncle Joe. Don't worry, Elliott."

"Because *you* know . . . the last thing I'd . . ."

"Forget it," said Father, and laughed again. "Why, Winston will have forgotten all about it when he wakes up."

But I don't think he ever did forget it. All the months I was to be stationed in England, later on, I was never again invited to spend the night at Chequers. Apparently Mr. Churchill never forgets.

And after that incident I was to appreciate all the more the effectiveness of Father's ability to keep those two men thinking along constructive and broadly similar lines. It was a job such as I would never hanker for.

Next day was also the P.M.'s birthday—his sixty-ninth —and there was to be a grand and fancy party in his honor at the British Embassy in the evening. So in the morning Father took advantage of the post exchange which had been established for his convenience in the Russian Embassy, to see if he could find anything appropriate for a present. Major General Connolly, commander of the Persian Gulf Command, had been able to stock the exchange with a fair display of Persian gifts; from among the knives, daggers, and rugs Father selected a bowl of some antiquity, and then went back to his apartment to receive Mohammed Reza Pahlevi, the young Shah of Persia, who had come to pay a formal protocol visit. He was accompanied by his Prime Minister, his Minister for Foreign Affairs, and also by Hussein Ala, then Minister of the Imperial Court. I had heard that the young Shah was quite a playboy; but for this occasion he was earnest, serious, and intent. He had brought a present, which father accepted on behalf of Mother, quite a handsome little rug. That formality out of the way, they settled down for a rather informal talk.

As ever, Father was interested in finding out more about the country, and in probing around for ideas that would help to solve its problems. He and the Iranian officials discussed the barren desert which made up such a great part of the country; they told him how, in centuries past, their land had been heavily wooded, and told of how it had become a dust bowl. This was a familiar subject to Father; warming up, he raised the question of a gigantic reforestation program; shifted from there to the plight of the majority of the Shah's subjects; tied the two things together; and was at length drawn by his visitors to a consideration of the economic grip which Britain had on Iran's oil wells and mineral deposits. Father nodded sympathetically, and agreed that steps should be taken to safeguard Iran's natural wealth. And when they had taken their leave, he beckoned me over.

"I want you to do something for me, Elliott. Go find Pat Hurley, and tell him to get to work drawing up a draft memorandum guaranteeing Iran's independence and her self-determination of her economic interests. I don't know exactly when I'll be able to see him, but try and find a time, will you, when you can slip him in to see me? I want to talk more to him about it."

I wasn't able to locate General Hurley before lunch, at which time Father was host to Stalin, Churchill, and their respective interpreters, but right after the others left, Hurley and I managed to steal a few of Father's minutes. Father explained what it was he wanted; Hurley acknowledged the request briefly, and was off.

"Need more men like him," Father commented, when he had gone. "I want you to stand by to give him any help he wants. An agreement from the Russians and the British guaranteeing Iranian sovereignty and political independence . . . it should be a good example of what we'll be able to accomplish, later on. I wish I had more men like Pat, on whom I could depend. The men in the State Department, those career diplomats . . . half the time I can't tell whether I should believe them or not."

The final meeting of the American, British, and Russian chiefs of staff was scheduled for four o'clock, and Father, the P.M., and Uncle Joe all attended. For a few minutes, while their discussions were going on, I stepped out on the balcony which overlooked the high room with its round table; constantly, around this balcony, Russian guard officers moved about, quietly and watchfully. Below, spread before me, was the proof of our united effort and our combined might: the same twelve Americans, the same eleven Britishers, the same five Russians as at the last plenary session, talking quietly, forcefully, meeting each other's arguments, coming to final agreement.

When they adjourned at six-fifteen I joined Father again, while he rested before Churchill's projected birthday party.

"It's settled at last," Father said, happily. "And," he added wrily, "for the fourth time. The western invasion is set. Even the date."

"The spring?" I asked.

"The first of May. Auspicious for the Russians: that's their big holiday, you know." Father was vastly relieved that this—as he hoped and thought—final decision had been reached, and the weight and timing of the all-out Allied effort finally buttoned up. Only the question of command was still in the air, but Father and the P.M. had promised Stalin that even this last detail would be decided upon in the extremely near future—they meant within the fortnight, if possible before they left Cairo the second time.

"And we agreed, too, that there should be a thrust up from the Mediterranean," Father added.

"Through the Balkans after all?" I asked, incredulous.

"No. Through southern France. Everything will be timed simultaneously—from the west, from the south, and the Russians from the east. I still say the end of 1944 will see the end of the war in Europe. Nobody can see how—with a really concerted drive from all sides—the Nazis can hold out much over nine months after we hit 'em."

A little after eight, dressed in evening clothes and holding the Persian bowl which was his birthday gift,

Father moved from the Soviet to the British Embassy, pleasant in the cool of the evening, flanked by its lily-pad pool, and guarded by turbaned Indian soldiers. This party was to be the top social event of our stay in Teheran, and the tone was being set in the British Embassy's reception room. Amid the glitter and the braid, I noticed that Captain Randolph Churchill had now joined his father's entourage. We wished our "happy birthdays" to the P.M.; he was absolutely in his element, jovial, beaming with good cheer, wreathed in smiles and cigar smoke. Father presented his bowl, together with the thought: "May we be together for many years." Cocktail glasses clinked and the air buzzed with friendly talk. Presently Stalin entered, together with Molotov and Voroshilov, and followed by his interpreter, Berezhkov; he was in time to sip two cocktails before we all moved in to dinner—thirty marshals, generals, admirals, ambassadors, ministers, diplomats, and lesser officials following the Prime Minister, the President, and the Marshal—and the one lady of the party, Sarah Oliver.

Of the dinner the night before, Father had later jokingly remarked that there had seemed to be three hundred and sixty-five toasts—one for every day in the year. At the P.M.'s birthday dinner, once more the Russian custom—everyone toasting everyone else—was observed, and once again I am afraid that accurate count was lost. I do remember that a good part of the dinner was spent standing up; I do remember Stalin's cheerful habit of touching the glass of everyone in whose name we were drinking; I do remember some of the toasts themselves.

Stalin: "My fighting friend Churchill!" and later, "My fighting friend Roosevelt!"

Churchill: "Stalin the mighty!" and "Roosevelt the President—my friend!"

And Father: "To our unity—war and peace!"

The occasion for toasting finding us all on our feet, several times some of us would remain standing, talking to each other; I remember listening at one point in between toasts to something Randolph Churchill had on his mind, of high import, I forget exactly what. And then there was one moment, when the gods of friendliness and good cheer were nodding, and General Sir Alan Brooke was on his feet, remarking on how the British people had suffered more in the war than any other, had lost more, had fought more, had done more to win the war; and a shadow of irritation was crossing Stalin's face. It may have been that moment—it probably was—that provoked him almost immediately afterward to rise to his feet in turn.

"I want to tell you, from the Soviet point of view, what the President and the United States have done to win the war. The most important things in this war are machines. The United States has proven that it can turn out from eight to ten thousand airplanes a month. England turns out three thousand a month, principally heavy bombers. The United States, therefore, is a country of machines. Without the use of those machines, through Lend-Lease, we would lose this war."

And Father, in his turn, paid tribute to the huge Red Army that was using those machines and, while we dined, rolling the Nazi war-machine steadily back toward its own homeland.

Next day I was scheduled to leave, to fly back to duty in Tunis. Before I left, however, I spent a few minutes with Father and Pat Hurley, going over what Pat—with rather insignificant assistance from me—had been able to draw up in the way of a three-power declaration covering Iran. The agreement was to be signed later in the day, if the Soviet Union and Great Britain concurred in its terms. Father studied the draft, nodded his head in agreement with it, and then looked up at Pat with a twinkle in his eye.

"By the way, Pat," he said, "where's your other star?"

"Sir?" asked Hurley, surprised.

"Your other star," Father repeated. "You've been promoted. The Congress has already approved it. Nobody notify you? You're a major general!"

And that was how Pat Hurley found out.

Before lunchtime, I said goodbye to Father. He had planned originally to stay over in Teheran until Friday, but the weather experts had told Major Otis Bryan that a cold front was passing Cairo which could be expected to fill the mountain passes by then; so Father had asked the Russians and British to readjust their schedules to permit him to get away that night. He wanted, if possible, to visit at least two of our military installations in Iran before returning to Cairo. He told me that he looked forward to about ten solid hours of political discussions with Stalin and Churchill, beginning at noon. It was a grueling schedule for him, especially as he was showing the signs of fatigue already, of the twenty-one days of his traveling and conferring.

"I don't know exactly when I'll be able to see you in Cairo, Pop," I said, "or even *if* I will."

"Try to get there, if only for a day or so."

"And if I don't, I'll probably see you again when you come through Tunis, won't I? So this is just goodbye for a few days. See you soon."

Leon Gray and Sgt. Cram were waiting for me at the field. We were in Cairo that night, and in Tunis the following night.

From the Log of the President's Trip:

Father left Teheran at ten-thirty Wednesday night, after the ten solid hours he had predicted, to spend the night at our Camp Amirabad, at the foot of the Elbruz Mountains. Next day, to the soldier-patients in the post hospital, and to the personnel at the camp, Father spoke impromptu.

"I have had conferences with Marshal Stalin and Mr. Churchill during the past four days—very successful too—laying military plans for cooperation between the three nations looking toward the winning of the war just as fast as we possibly can, and I think we have made progress. . . .

"The other purpose was to talk over world conditions after the war—to try to plan a world for us and for our children when war would cease to be a necessity. We have made great progress in that also. . . .

"And so I am on my way home. I wish I could take all of you with me. . . ."

His plane circled low over Baghdad. He was back at Ambassador Kirk's villa in Cairo a little after three o'clock on Thursday. That morning, the official story of the First Cairo Conference had been released.

8

CAIRO II

THE JOB THAT had called me back to Tunis from Teheran was that of closing out our rear headquarters at La Marsa and flying it north to Italy. The last of the twenty-eight hundred men and officers in the outfit were on their way by the weekend, so I was able to fly back to Cairo again for a brief visit. I knew that sessions of the Combined Chiefs of Staff had been resumed there immediately following the return from Teheran four or five days earlier; I knew, too, that Father and the P.M. planned to invite Ismet Inonu, Turkey's president, down to Cairo for some conversations.

In Tunis, I had the opportunity for a brief chat with General Eisenhower; his concern over the possibility he would have to take over a Pentagon job was still evident; he knew no more than anyone else of the final decisions about command of OVERLORD. That OVERLORD was definitely scheduled, that the Russians had sided with us against any further exploitation of the Mediterranean theater and against bringing Turkey into the war, I was able to tell him, pretty definitely.

Early on Sunday, December 5th, I took off for Cairo, again with Leon Gray, and by the late afternoon we were settling down at the ATC field once more. I went directly to the Kirk villa where I knew Father would again be staying. Inside, I ran into John Boettiger, who told me that there had been an amusing diplomatic contest between the P.M. and Father: both had dispatched planes to Adana, in Turkey, to bring President Inonu back to Cairo; John had been Father's emissary, and he had won. How important it was that the Turkish president should arrive in an American Army plane rather than a British, nobody seemed to know, but John was pleased, nevertheless.

I found Father in bed, reading a detective story. He had had a full day, what with one plenary meeting of the Combined Chiefs, two hours of conversations with Inonu, Churchill, and their respective advisers, and then another meeting with the American Joint Chiefs. He had given a dinner for Inonu the night before; this Sunday night Churchill was planning a second one, to which Father would have to go. Now he was resting for it, but he put down his "whodunit" to talk to me when I came in. He commented on the load of business still before him that was going to keep him in Cairo until Tuesday morning, when they had originally hoped to leave late Sunday night.

"I'll be glad to get home," he said, and laughed. "After only a month! I should think of the men who haven't been home since before Pearl Harbor!"

"Doesn't seem like only a month, somehow."

"A lot's happened. Especially the last week."

I asked him about the last day at Teheran.

"Have you seen the communiqué we agreed on?" he asked, and when I shook my head, he pointed to some papers on a table. A copy of the communiqué was on top, and I read it through once very quickly, and then more slowly, while Father threw in comments. It was, he said, chiefly his language, and purposely not in the usual careful diplomatic phrases; ". . . banish war for many generations," I read, and pointed to it on the page. " 'Many generations,' " I said. "Why not 'forever'?"

"Two wars in two generations," Father answered. "The people of the world have heard, in the last quarter-century, too many people who promised them peace 'forever.' We agreed at Teheran that our three countries, the three strongest countries in the world, could be intelligent enough about future disagreements, could so unify our foreign policies as to ensure that there would be no war 'for many generations.' That's what we talked about, from noon until ten o'clock—how to unify our policies, how to mesh our individual nations' interests in the interests of a general security for the whole world.

"And in between times, Uncle Joe and I had a few words, too, just the two of us." He sighed comfortably and stretched, as though dismissing the subject. Obviously, though, that was too tantalizing a moment to break it off, and he saw that on my face. "Well, there were some more aspects of the picture in the Far East that I'd wanted to talk to him about . . . you were there, weren't you, when we started talking about it?"

"The first time I met him."

"That's right. Well"—he yawned, interrupting himself—"we still had an area of agreement to arrive at, and once he'd agreed to enter the war against Japan, I . . ."

"*What?*"

"Sure. He talked about the war in the Pacific . . . oh, it must have been while you were still in Teheran."

"But, that's terrific! Why didn't you tell me?"

He grinned. "You never asked me, as the tattooed lady said on her wedding night."

"When are they getting in? How soon?"

"Oh, not for months yet, anyway. I think he offered to declare war against Japan and start fighting in the Far East in order to win finally the argument for a second front in the west. He was willing to get in as soon as he could get troops to Siberia, if we would just promise the May first invasion in the west. But after all, it makes more sense, militarily, to have the Russians bringing all their weight against Hitler on an eastern front. Time enough for him to fight against Japan after Hitler's licked."

I was still too startled by the information to say anything.

"So," Father went on, "he's agreed that as soon as he can get supplies and troops across to Siberia—across the one railroad—he'll declare war against Japan. He mentioned a time period, too: six months after the final defeat of Hitler.

"Anyway, in view of that, there was quite a lot I wanted to talk to him about: China after the war, the Chinese Communists, and so on. Couldn't do a lot of that talking while Winston was around, because a lot of it had to do with British extraterritorial rights in Hong Kong, Canton, and Shanghai . . . how if we agreed to support Chiang against the British on that point, he would agree to form a really democratic government in China. And Chiang was worried about what the Russians would do in Manchuria, too . . . although I don't think he'll be so worried now. Uncle Joe agreed that of course Manchuria would remain with the Chinese and agreed to help us back Chiang against the British. . . . And Pat Hurley has gone on to Moscow to carry our talks further."

This reminded me that I had had a minor part to play in the drafting and negotiating of the three-power agreement on Iran's future. I asked Father if it had been signed, eventually.

"Oh, yes. Signed, sealed, and delivered. And, by the way, thanks for what *you* did. That Pat Hurley . . ." Father went on, ruminatively. "He did a good job. If anybody can straighten out the mess of internal Chinese politics, he's the man. You know, Elliott," he said, throwing off a quilt and preparing to get up, "men like Pat Hurley are invaluable. Why? Because they're loyal. I can give him assignments that I'd *never* give a man in the State Department, because I can depend on him. You know what I mean?"

I was thinking about State Department men who had got Father into situations from which he had had to extricate himself.

"You know," Father was saying, "any number of times the men in the State Department have tried to conceal messages to me, delay them, hold them up somehow, just because some of those career diplomats aren't in accord with what they know I think. They should be working for Winston. As a matter of fact, a lot of the time, they *are*. Stop to think of 'em: any number of 'em are convinced that the way for America to conduct its foreign policy is to find out what the British are doing, and then copy that. It isn't a question of whether they're Democrats or Republicans," Father said, angrily warming to his subject. "As far as I know, Pat Hurley and a half-dozen others who work for me are dyed-in-the-wool Republicans. But they know their country's at war, and they're anxious to do what they can for their country. So they do it." Arthur Prettyman had come in, and was helping him dress. "I was told," Father said, "six years ago, to clean out that State Department. It's like the British Foreign Office. They have a man there, his title is Permanent Under-Secretary. He's Permanent Under-Secretary if the Government is Tory, or if it's Labor, or if it's Liberal. Makes no difference. There he is: Permanent. That's our State Department. So: there are men like Pat Hurley, and what they do is twice as valuable. The only thing about Pat is, he has to be told what to do. If he's told, he'll do it. And he'll do it faithfully and well. He will, too." He stopped, grinning at the way he himself had started raising his voice. "Say," he said, "I'm supposed to have been resting. It's *your* fault for getting me thinking about those State Department striped-pants boys."

I laughed, and he asked me why I wasn't dressing for dinner too. I told him I had not been invited, and that furthermore even if I had been asked I did not intend to go. "I'm tired, Pop. I've been working hard, too. And I didn't get to bed last night. I'm just going to grab a bite here and get to bed."

He looked enviously at me. "But you'll be around to-morrow?"

"Oh, sure. Until four or five o'clock anyway."

And in the morning, when I saw him again, he told me that the question of Turkey's entry into the war had been finally decided upon. Against.

"In a sense, I guess, it was Winston's last effort to force an allied attack from the south, from the Mediterranean," he said.

I asked him whether Russia had taken any position, and he smiled.

"They agreed with me. No Lend-Lease to Turkey, said Stalin, in effect, if it means any delay on the western front. Winston and I are going to draw up some sort of statement to save Turkey's face this afternoon. After all, it's been in the newspapers for nearly a month now that she was going to declare war against Germany on our side."

I wagged my head, thinking about how well Stalin and Father had got along, thinking about the identity of interests that we apparently had. And when I said something to that effect:

"The biggest thing," Father commented, "was in making clear to Stalin that the United States and Great Britain were not allied in one common bloc against the Soviet Union. I think we've got rid of that idea, once and for all. I hope so. The one thing that could upset the applecart, after the war, is if the world is divided again, Russia against England and us. That's our big job now, and it'll be our big job tomorrow, too: making sure that we continue to act as referee, as intermediary between Russia and England."

And in doing that, it was clear, the United States had become world leader. No longer was our foreign policy simply tailing after Britain's: Father had been successful in demonstrating over the conference table that we were independent of our English-speaking cousins, that our function would be to integrate, in the future organization of the United Nations, the disparate views of the Empire-minded British and the Communist-minded Russians. How this would or would not work out in practice remained for history to reveal, but I can set it down that in Cairo, having come from the Teheran Conference, Father was convinced it would work out smoothly for all parties concerned, not the least of which were the small nations of the world.

After he left me, his Monday morning was given over to work on official mail from Washington. Around noon, General Stilwell came in; it would be the last time he saw Stilwell; they had twenty or more minutes together, during which Vinegar Joe voiced his dissatisfaction with the politics of the Generalissimo, and made the point that Chiang was storing up all his strength to use against the Chinese Communists after the war. Father, his mind on his agreement with Chiang and his subsequent agreement with Stalin, said little, beyond urging that Stilwell work things out as best he could. It was clear that Father, throughout his talk with Stilwell, had other things on his mind; personally, I believe he was going over again mentally the need for first crushing the Nazis, only after which would he allow himself to give priority to the problems the American command in China faced.

At lunch, with Churchill and Harry Hopkins as Father's only guests, the talk was of the forthcoming communiqué covering Inonu's visit. The language of the communiqué had to be delicately arrived at, in view of the continued hostility between Turkey and the Soviet Union, especially inasmuch as Churchill had been hoping Turkey would become a fighting ally in the war. Inonu himself came in after we had left the lunch table, and shortly thereafter the others were joined by Vinogradov, the Soviet Ambassador to Turkey, representing Stalin. The communiqué to be drafted had to make clear that the Turkish government was in agreement with those of the Soviet Union, Great Britain, and the United States, despite the fact that Turkey would not be entering the war as had been forecast by the most perspicacious journalists. This was what led to words like: "the firm friendship existing between the Turkish Republic, the United States of America, and the Soviet Union," and "the strength of the alliance which united Great Britain and Turkey."

The communiqué was formalized, and the farewells made, after which Father moved out to the rear steps of the Kirk villa, to talk impromptu to a detachment of MP's who had been guarding the delegates to the conference. From inside the door I listened, as he said:

". . . . This time when we clean out the enemy we are

going to clean them out thoroughly, so that they can't start another war. . . . Even if we have to keep peace by force for a while, we are going to do it. . . ."

He sounded cheerful; there was no question of his optimism, after the hard days that lay behind him.

When he was through, I again had to say a temporary goodbye; I was anxious to get started back to Tunis before nightfall. I stayed until just before General MacArthur's Chief of Staff, Sutherland, was ushered in, and in those few moments I had alone with him I learned that once again he and Winston Churchill were divided, and over another issue. The subject came up when I mentioned idly that I had seen Eisenhower in Tunis, and would probably be seeing him again the next morning.

"Say hello for me," said Father. "He'll be taking on an even bigger job pretty soon; poor fellow, I don't envy him."

Poor Ike, I thought; so it's back to the Pentagon for him, after all.

"Is that official, Pop? Can I say anything to him about it, if I see him or Butcher?"

"It's not absolutely settled yet, Elliott. But it seems pretty clear that Winston will refuse absolutely to let Marshall take over. Marshall . . . it's not that he's argued too often with the P.M. on military matters, it's just that he's won too often. It's a disappointment for him, too, I'm sure."

I could not figure out what Father meant for a moment. "You mean Ike *won't* be going back to the Pentagon?"

"The way it looks now, he's got the biggest field job cut out for him anybody ever had. What would he be doing in the Pentagon?"

On my way to the ATC field to start the flight back to Tunis, I thought about the decision to put Eisenhower in command of OVERLORD, as it now seemed probable would happen. Of course, it was good news for Ike, but I was thinking about George Marshall. From all that Father had said, from all that I had overheard, at the conferences as far back as Argentia, from the conduct of the war itself, it was quite obvious that Marshall's qualities were something quite special, made of him a commander —whether on staff or in the field—unusually well equipped to handle men, to run a war, to run a conference table. And—to his own disappointment—they seemed to be also qualities which had made him an enemy in Winston Churchill. I remembered what Father had said to me at Teheran, about Marshall being the only American general that was able doggedly to carry his point with the P.M., against the P.M. But, I reminded myself, the ability to get along unflaggingly with Churchill was also quite a quality: and this Eisenhower had demonstrated over and over again he had. This, too, would be of paramount importance, in any invasion based on England.

When Father's plane put down at El Aouina in Tunis, the following afternoon, General Eisenhower, General Spaatz, Harry Butcher, and I were on hand to greet him and his party. In the car from the airport back to the "White House" at Carthage, he poured out his interest in his day's flight to me and General Eisenhower. Major Otis Bryan had taken him right along the coast, right over the path of the Nazis' retreat in front of Montgomery: he had had a perfect view of one battlefield after another; he had seen from the plane the wreckage of the Nazi Afrika Korps, spilled out across the desert over a thousand miles and more, planes and tanks and trucks. El Alamein was succeeded by Tobruk, and in turn by Benghazi, Tripoli, and Sfax; Father was as excited as though he had himself commanded the British Eighth Army.

In the few hours I had had at Carthage before Father's arrival, I had been busy lining up a dinner mess. We ate at Father's villa, but the food was a strictly GI affair, except for the waiters. The waiters were two Italian prisoners. And the dinner itself was to celebrate the majority of one of the officers in my outfit, David Brooks, from Oklahoma City. I doubt that ever a young officer had such a company present to celebrate his promotion: besides the Commander-in-Chief, there were five generals, among them the Allied commander and the commander of the American Air Forces in the Mediterranean, and three admirals, Leahy, McIntire, and Brown. I suspect that the Secret Service men in Father's party were a little nervous about our Italian waiters; there were gimlet eyes boring into the backs of those two unfortunates throughout dinner; but they were not out to poison anybody, only to marvel that they were permitted in the same room with a chief of state. Trembling, they shook hands with Father after dinner; later, still goggle-eyed, they confessed to me that they would have thought it impossible to get so close to Mussolini or Victor Emmanuel, for even in prewar Italy they would have been regarded as potential enemies of the state.

After dinner, there was only opportunity for me to discover that in fact Eisenhower had been finally decided upon as leader of the combined operation invading France. Father said his notification would come from Marshall, who was still in Cairo, and that Ike was under no circumstances to hear of it until then. Father was quite tired that night, almost completely at the limit of his strength; and yet there was still a tour of inspection for him to encompass. In fact, he was anxious to extend the tour beyond Malta and Sicily, which were scheduled, into Italy; but General Eisenhower again put his foot down, refusing permission, disclaiming responsibility.

Tired though he was, there was a quiet jubilance in his manner. He was a man who knew he had accomplished a great deal, on a limited mission.

He was up before me, the next morning, and off by C-54, with a fighter escort, to Malta ("Under repeated fire from the skies, Malta stood, alone but unafraid in the center of the sea, one tiny bright flame in the darkness—a beacon for the clearer days which have come"), and then to Sicily (where Mark Clark was awarded a DSC, completely to his surprise; he had had no idea why he had been ordered down from Italy). I was on hand to greet him again at El Aouina when he got back, at four-thirty, and our dinner at eight was attended only by his staff: Leahy, Brown, McIntire, Pa Watson, and me.

The only thing that I wanted to find out from him, before he took off next morning for home, he was of course in no position to tell me. I wanted to know whether Tooey Spaatz was going to England with Ike, because from that I would be able to get an idea as to whether my outfit would have a chance at the invasion. Father's information, however, stopped at about the second echelon from the top, and Spaatz's job was not part of that rare atmosphere. And anyway, the only thing that Father wanted to talk about, that last evening, was the cornerstone accomplishment of his month away from home.

"The United Nations . . ." he said to me that last night, with great satisfaction. "People at home, Congressmen, editorial writers, talk about the United Nations as something which exists only on account of war. The tendency is to snipe at it by saying that only because we are forced into unity by war are we unified. But war isn't the real force to unity. *Peace* is the real force. *After* the war—*then* is when I'm going to be able to make sure the United Nations are really the United Nations!"

Up at six the next morning, to motor to the airport. Father was headed by plane to Dakar, where he would board the *Iowa,* and start for a Christmas at home. I was going back with the last planeload of men and officers from my rear headquarters north to San Severo, in Italy, where we would spend a cold and muddy Christmas wondering if we were to stay in Italy for the duration, or if we would be among the fortunate who would carry the war home to the Nazis, by May first of 1944.

9

FROM CAIRO-TEHERAN TO YALTA

THERE WAS NOTHING approaching top-level about my weeks in Italy immediately following the last sessions of the conference at Cairo. About as discreetly as any soldier from the rank of yardbird up, I tried to pump the ever-flowing wells of scuttle-butt, in an effort to find out whether my outfit would rate an assignment to the United Kingdom. At about the time when the word was beginning to trickle through that the chances looked worse than usual—which meant, from Army experience, that they looked better than usual—we heard the disturbing rumor that an "end run" was planned around the Nazi defenses across Italy to some point on the western coast close to Rome. This was to be the Anzio beachhead, and I could not believe that such an adventure was being taken seriously, after what I had learned of the strategy hammered out by the Combined Chiefs in Egypt and subsequently in Iran.

Before there were any last-minute preparations for this adventure, however, I got orders to report to General

Spaatz's headquarters in England. And on arrival I was told my duties: to reorganize all the American Reconnaissance Air Forces units of both the Eighth (bombardment, strategic) and Ninth (light bombardment, tactical) Air Forces, and to supervise their operations so as to obtain all information necessary to the invasion of Europe. Shortly thereafter I heard the news of the Anzio landings. But was not until several weeks later, when I happened to spend some time with General Eisenhower, that I learned of how the P.M. had personally insisted on this plan, which he code-named SHINGLE, and which was apparently his last—highly individual, resolutely high-handed—attempt to force invasion of Europe via the south rather than the west.

My outfit joined the swelling ranks of American soldiers in Britain on January 19th, and we promptly went to work beside our British opposites of the RAF. In view of the criticisms which I have expressed in regard to some of the British warmakers, I am anxious to set it down that these RAF officers with whom I worked from mid-January up until D-Day and thereafter until the final Nazi capitulation were a group of consummately knowledgeable officers, thoroughly familiar with their job and individually and severally as hardworking and as anxious to win the war as quickly as possible as any group of men it would have been possible to find. Not only were they a constant credit to their country, but they were in large part responsible for the small percentage of losses suffered in the invasion itself. I know I speak for all the American officers who worked with RAF reconnaissance experts in according them a considerable amount of the credit for the success of our arms in Europe.

January, February, March; and in April there came the first tangible evidence that a plan which had been discussed at Teheran, for shuttle-bombing between England and the Soviet Union, and Italy and the Soviet Union, was going to bear fruit. A Soviet general arrived at SHAEF, carried on some preparatory conversations, and then returned. And then in May I got word that I was to accompany Generals Fred Anderson and Ted Curtis and some staff officers of the Eighth Air Force to Russia to have a look at the airfields which had been tentatively assigned us, and to settle all final details before the shuttle operations should begin. It was good news that the Russians were agreeable to the shuttle-bombing plan, that they were figuring on giving our bombers fighter support, and especially that they had announced they would permit air reconnaissance photography. It was this last, of course, that involved me in the trip.

The flight took me through some familiar places: Casablanca, Tunis, Cairo, Teheran (where we took on a Red Army navigator and a Red Army radio operator), and then on to Moscow. This was the first of two wartime trips I made to Russia; we were there only a little over a week, so my impressions are necessarily somewhat sketchy, but nevertheless quite vivid. I remember Moscow's wide, wide avenues; and the banquet tendered us by some high-ranking Red Air Force officers, where I was placed between two Russians, and our conversation was almost exclusively pantomime; I remember the Kremlin, where we went to call on Molotov—a vast building that dwarfs even our Pentagon, and seemed unlike any office building I had ever seen, what with thick red carpets lining its hallways, and the comfortable furniture of its suites; I remember the magnificent opera house, where we saw Rimsky-Korsakoff's *The Snow Maiden,* infinitely more beautiful, more handsomely staged, better sung than a performance of the same opera I had once attended in our own Metropolitan Opera in New York City; and I remember the audience at the opera—ninety per cent uniformed, but not without a scattering of elegantly gowned women. And then there was a dinner at the Moscow Hotel with the American correspondents, seven of them; they told me in the limited time available a little about the country they were assigned to cover: how a dinner like the one we were eating was costing their publishers the tidy sum of nearly $700, yet the regular Russian ration cost only some five dollars a month, the purpose being to discourage eating in hotels and restaurants; how a ranking officer or a ranking ballet star or writer or scientist could get what he or she needed at a fifty or seventy-five per cent price reduction; how, for the Russians, an all-out war effort meant an all-out war effort, *period.*

And I remember our flying inspection of the fields assigned for our shuttle operations, especially the one at Poltava, which before the war had been equivalent to our Randolph Field in Texas, and was, at the time we saw it, still little more than the shambles the Nazis had left when they retreated. It was there that I first saw elements of the Red Army at work, and learned to respect the vigor with which they overcame obstacles. Building an airfield, for them, meant using at manual labor hundreds and thousands of ex-combat troops, men who had been wounded, to do what in America a dozen rollers and a dozen scrapers and two dozen ground crewmen could take care of. Yet they were getting the job done, and amazingly well and quickly. Russian women were doing this work, too: husky Amazons who thought nothing of tossing around fifty-gallon gasoline drums like toys.

From the air we saw the forthright way in which the Red Army solved the question of supply and transport: lacking hard-surfaced roads their trucks took out across country, and when the path got too muddy and sticky they fanned out to either side of the original tracks, until their passage could be marked by a great four- or five-hundred-yard-wide swath cut into the steppes. A one-track railroad fed supplies to the entire southern Soviet front; when our shuttle operations began we insisted on moving in our own 100-octane aviation gasoline and bombs from the Persian Gulf, and thereby snafued their transport; but they cheerfully granted us the permission.

We carried away the impression that the Russians were almost childishly eager to get along with us, cooperate with us; for every Red Air Force officer who insisted he was too busy to see us until after ten o'clock at night, and made us hang around cooling our heels, there were a dozen who made abundantly clear the respect that they had for Americans and for American machines and for American industrial efficiency. Joe Davies demonstrated how simple the job of cooperation with the Russians is; it is a tragedy that our own Government has not seen fit to assign more men like Davies to the critical job of representing us in the Soviet Union.

Back in London after this mission to Moscow and the southern Russian front, I had one opportunity for relaxation from the constantly growing pressure of the imminent invasion. This was an evening of bridge, with Ted Curtis and I going down in ignominious defeat before the deadly efficiency of Ike Eisenhower, who teamed that night with his aide, Harry Butcher. I remember the occasion because they pumped us dry about our trip to the Soviets. What was it like? What was their army like? How were their fliers? How was their discipline? What did they think of us? They were interested not so much in the attitudes of the officials who had turned up at Teheran or in London as in those of the field officers, and the Russian GI's. And when we had answered their questions as well as we could:

"The big thing for all of them," I said, "is still the second front. That's the one big test of what they think of us. If it comes off, okay. If not . . ."

"If?" growled Eisenhower. "What's this 'if'?"

I told him that I was thinking about the commitment Father and the P.M. had made, back at Teheran, and the date, May first.

"I don't know about those commitments. I wasn't there. But I know about the invasion of France. The Russians needn't worry about that one."

D-Day. Overlord and the well-timed simultaneous Soviet push. The V-1's and the V-2's. I read in the *Stars and Stripes* about the meeting at Dumbarton Oaks, and was made happy to think that the Big Three were so far along in their unity on the problems of the peace. A letter from Father, a brief one, told me something about the meeting with the P.M. in Quebec, that September, at which the principal point on the agenda had been the war against Japan. My days and nights, during the summer and fall of 1944, were exclusively occupied with the affairs of photographic reconnaissance over France and Germany and the Lowlands; and the work was exhausting and concentrated enough so that I was delighted when word came that I was to be sent back to the States on a technical mission. That meant assignment to the Pentagon; that meant Washington; that meant seeing Father and the family again.

My sister Anna was the first member of the family to meet me, in the White House, and she told me something of what to expect when I saw Father. Nevertheless, I was still a little startled, principally because there had been so much talk about how unwell he was, in the campaign just recently completed. He looked tired and thin, but that was all.

"What'd you expect?" he asked, sticking out his hand, when I had wangled a brief visit, sandwiched in between two appointments. "These campaign trips get a little tougher, but I thrive on 'em!"

He looked older, he looked tired. But there was color in his cheeks. He told me he was hoping to get away, perhaps to Warm Springs, for one or two weeks, and that most certainly he was looking forward to a Christmas at Hyde Park. "Would you like that?" he asked.

"Sure, I would. But how do I know where I'll be? I'll probably be back in England, by then. Depends on my job."

I asked him when I would get a chance to spend some time with him, finding out what had been going on since I had last seen him in Africa, nearly a year before.

"I'm the one wants to do the finding out," he answered. "I want to find out all about the war, first-hand, from you." He looked at his pad, scratched his pencil through something, and announced that he could make it that very night. "After dinner. If you get a chance, read some of the newspapers this afternoon. I think that's the best way there is for you to find out how close the country thinks we are to victory."

I did not remind him of his prediction, a year ago, that we would have beaten the Nazis by the end of 1944. But I did have a chance to read some of the newspapers and news magazines, and that night I referred to them.

"I see what you mean, Pop. They're all talking about Europe, *after* the war. Talking about how there's not enough Big Three unity, and why don't you call another Big Three meeting."

He nodded. "I guess it's a question of their wanting *something* to be critical about. And fortunately the war is being won."

I asked him if another meeting of the Big Three was in the cards.

"Oh, there'll have to be one, all right. I hope we'll be able to get together some time late in January, soon after the inauguration. Actually, the only question is where. Stalin is anxious that it be somewhere in Russia."

"Again?"

"Well, you know, it's hard to refuse. He *is* in charge of the Red Army, and the Red Army *is* on the go."

That first night, true to his threat, he made me do most of the talking—whatever I could report about the war and the way we were fighting it he drank in thirstily. He kept me in his bedroom until late, pumping me with one question after another, until it was too late for me to turn the tables and ask him one or two.

Two or three mornings later, though, I got my chance, when the general to whom I was to report at the Pentagon sent word he would not be able to see me until the next day. I promptly headed for the White House, and Father's room, hoping to catch him before he started his day's work. He waved me to a chair; he was scowling over some official dispatches; the morning newspapers had been irritably crumpled on the floor. For some minutes he read, exclaiming every now and then, muttering his dissatisfaction. When he looked up, my eyebrows were raised in curiosity.

"Greece," he said. "British troops. Fighting against the guerrillas who fought the Nazis for the last four years." He made no attempt to conceal his anger. I had seen only a vague and obviously incomplete story in one of the Washington papers; the complete story would not be printed for some weeks to come. "How the British can dare such a thing!" Father cried. "The lengths to which they will go to hang on to the past!" Beside him, his coffee was brewing; he glanced at it, noted that it was ready, and poured himself a cup, looking over to me with an invitation to join him. "I've got an extra cup here," he said.

"Fine!"

"I wouldn't be surprised," he went on, "if Winston had simply made it clear he was backing the Greek Royalists. That would be only in character. But killing Greek guerrillas! Using British soldiers for such a job!"

"Probably using American Lend-Lease equipment to do it, too," I reminded him.

"I'll find out about *that*," Father said. And then, "Though I don't suppose there's too much I can do about it."

"A public statement?"

"Condemning the British?" He shook his head. "Not now. Time enough to raise it when I see Winston in February. And anyway . . ." and his scowl disappeared.

"Anyway what?"

He changed the subject, abruptly. "You know, it was just about a year ago that Queen Wilhelmina was here. In the White House. For a visit. And we got to talking" —he grinned—"I should say, I got *her* to talking, about the Dutch colonies, and what was going to happen to them after the war. Java, Borneo—all the Netherlands East Indies. Talked back and forth for more than six hours, over two or three evenings. I made the point that it was American arms that would be liberating those colonies from the Japanese. American soldiers and sailors and marines. I mentioned the Philippines." He grinned in recollection. "And, Elliott, she agreed that the policy we have in the Philippines would be the pattern she would follow in the Dutch East Indies, after the war. She promised me that her government would announce, immediately after victory in Japan, that they were going to grant the peoples of the Dutch East Indies first dominion status, with the right of self-rule and equality.

"Then, after their government has been established, if the people, by free vote, decide that they want complete independence, they shall be granted it. Just as we are granting it in the Philippines.

"That's a commitment. And it means a sharp break away from the leadership of the British. Think what that will mean to Stalin! How it will show him what the western nations can and will accomplish, in the postwar!"

I gathered that he had been reminded of these conversations with Queen Wilhelmina by British arrogance in Greece.

"That's right," he said. "That's right. That's why, for one thing, I don't think any public statement condemning the British actions in Greece is necessary, quite apart from what it would mean to the Axis, in terms of propaganda.

"The point is that we are going to be able to bring pressure on the British to fall in line with *our* thinking, in relation to the *whole* colonial question. It's all tied up in the one package: the Dutch East Indies, French Indo-China, India, British extraterritorial rights in China. . . . We're going to be able to make this the twentieth century after all, you watch and see!"

His sharp irritation of a few minutes before had disappeared completely, as he contemplated with gusto his plans for the kind of foreign policy which would not only be independent of the British Foreign Office but would force that citadel of Empire to a recognition of progress.

And it was clear that he was looking forward to the rehashing of global policy at the proposed next meeting with his associates in the Big Three.

A few days later I left Washington, bound on personal business of a happy character. In Arizona, on December third, Faye Emerson and I were married. I had expected that I would be ordered back to the ETO after two or three weeks at most; but just before December sixteenth I was granted an unexpected and very welcome furlough —more exactly in Army parlance, I was told I would stay in the States on "temporary duty" until after Christmas. Those orders came through just before the sixteenth: it was on the sixteenth that Hitler launched his breakthrough in the Ardennes. When the news was flashed back to the Pentagon, I was flabbergasted. One of the principal functions of air reconnaissance is to gather precisely the sort of information which would enable field commanders to be on their guard and prepared for the sort of operation which—from the dispatches to the Pentagon and subsequently from the official communiqués—it was clear had caught us, if not with our pants down, at least with our belt pretty seriously loose. The breakthrough meant—I feared—that my outfit had been gravely remiss, and my immediate instinct was to put a request through channels asking permission to get on a plane back to SHAEF and find out what had gone wrong. My bosses, however, took the eminently sensible position that what had happened had happened, and that my absence or presence would have no appreciable effect on the fortunes of the breakthrough or its containing. Stuck, then, back in Washington, far from my outfit, I could only speculate on what had happened; weather was no excuse, for photographic reconnaissance is expected to bring back results in fair weather or foul. Only when my temporary duty in Washington was over, and I had flown back to the ETO, did I find that in fact our reconnaissance had been perfectly up to snuff, that the information on the massing of enemy troops behind the Ardennes had all been satisfactorily collated and passed on "through channels"—and then held up or ignored by an unthinking G-2 officer.

The last days of my stay we spent with my family at Hyde Park, the last Christmas which I was to share with Father. For a wonder, in view of the current headlines and the dominating fact of the war, it was a time of great peace and contentment; the world was for a brief moment shut out, and we were once more one family together, the more closely knit—as Father had pointed out, a year ago in Cairo, at Thanksgiving—because we were a big family.

The center table in the long living room was pushed back, the Christmas tree was in place and decorated, the piles of presents were ready for the unwrapping—each person's pile heaped on a separate chair. And on Christmas Eve Father took his accustomed rocker, to one side of the fireplace, and opened the familiar book, while we all found places around him. My place was prone on the floor, by the grate. The fire crackled pleasantly; Father's voice, going over the well-remembered *Christmas Carol,* rose and fell rhythmically; my thoughts wandered, aimless, and presently ceased altogether. Then, Jab!, in my ribs came Faye's elbow, and her fierce whisper in my ear: "You were snoring! Sit up!" and I looked up sheepishly at Father, who only winked at me gravely, and went on reading. I noticed that for some reason he had forgotten to put a false tooth in its place in the front of his lower jaw. So, all of a sudden, did my nephew, Chris, Franklin Junior's three-year-old son. He leaned forward and in a clear voice interrupted Father's reading. "Grandpère, you've lost a tooth!" It was a simple, direct statement, not requesting or requiring an answer, so Father smiled and went on reading. But all Chris' interest in *A Christmas Carol* was gone. Presently he stood up and walked over quite close to Father, leaned still closer, reached a pointing finger within inches, and insisted, "Grandpère, you've lost a tooth. Did you swallow it?"

And that ended *A Christmas Carol* for that evening. "There's too much competition in this family for reading aloud," Father laughed, and slammed shut the book.

"Next year," said my wife, "it'll be a peacetime Christmas. And we'll all listen as good as gold."

"Next year," said Mother, "next year we'll *all* be home again."

And on Christmas Day, after the presents had all been opened, and the wrapping paper gathered up, I went to the corner of the room where Father was sitting at his desk, carefully pasting one of his more gratefully received presents in a stamp album. Jokingly, I murmured something about a United Nations stamp which he would one day add to his collection.

"Don't think I won't, Elliott," he said. "And sooner than you think, too." He leaned back and waved his magnifying glass at me. "Funny thing, I was just thinking about a stamp like that. Maybe I'll have it put on the agenda, at the meeting next month." He laughed. "Or do you think they would suspect me of ulterior philatelic motives?"

"It's definite, then, for next month?"

"As definite as anything in this life. I'm looking forward to it, too. Change'll do me good."

"Any chance you'll be needing an aide?"

He smiled. "Depends on your commanders, Elliott. I hope it'll work out all right."

"So do I."

"But even if it shouldn't, I'll be seeing you soon again, anyway. I'm seriously thinking of a trip to England, in the late spring or early summer. I think that might well be the best way to sell the British people and the British Parliament on the need for Britain to put its hopes for the future in the United Nations—*all* the United Nations—and not just in the British Empire and British ability to get other countries to combine in some sort of bloc against the Soviet Union."

I asked him if he seriously thought there was some danger of that.

"It's what we've got to expect," he answered, very seriously. "It's what we've got to plan now to contend against." He paused, and then: "This is no talk for

Christmas." And Mother, coming up behind me, said firmly, "Just what I was going to say. We agreed, no talk of business today."

I put Faye on the train back to Hollywood, and in turn made my goodbyes to Father and Mother and the rest of the family two days later. I was back at my command with the New Year, and plunged back into work. After three weeks of it, I read in *Stars and Stripes* that Father was to have a simple inaugural ceremony, and was happy, thinking that Faye would be able to get back to Washington to be present for it. And then, ka-boom, the heavens opened up and I found myself involved in more wars than just that against the Nazis.

I see no useful purpose in taking up space to write about *L'Affaire* Blaze. If Faye had needed any introduction to the hazards of marrying into the Roosevelt family, she got it. The hot wind blew merrily on Capitol Hill. The Inspector General himself came down to my headquarters, expecting to find I do not know what. On top of all of which, with rare and diabolical timing, the War Department's list of men nominated to the grade of general officer was placed on Father's desk, and on it—having been put there by Doolittle and having been approved by Spaatz and Eisenhower—was my name.

Faye later told me that Father, although such lists were generally approved by him as a matter of routine course, really hesitated and thought not only twice but thrice. It had always been his practice to make his children fight their own battles. This time, however, I guess he permitted himself the luxury of losing his temper: he told my wife that he was convinced I rated the promotion, and that was that. Firmly he signed his approval of the list and sent it on to the Senate, and promptly he wrote me a letter telling me what he had done and explaining that he wanted the Senate to decide whether the confidence of my commanding general was justified. I stuck my fingers in my ears, and waited. Sure enough, another Congressional investigation.

But Blaze's evil star had not finished its work with me yet. Late in January Harry Hopkins arrived in France, and he looked me up at SHAEF, in Paris. I remember with gratitude the tactful way in which he broke the news to me. Casually he let fall the information that a Big Three meeting had been definitely set for Yalta, in the Crimea; that that was why he was on that side of the ocean. Then he remarked that Father was even at the moment, as he spoke to me, on his way over, aboard the *Quincy,* and accompanied by a task force. Seeing that I was about to pop the crucial question, he speeded up his tempo just a bit. Father had wanted me to act as aide again, he said, but had hesitated to put in a request for my services at the War Department. Father, Harry said, did not want to have the War Department put in that kind of a spot, since it seemed fairly clear that the Republicans on the Hill would scream to the skies.

It was a disappointment. Then, in his next breath, Harry said that Father was bringing my sister Anna along with him. Sure enough, I began to feel better: I knew that Pop liked to have a member of the family along, somebody with whom he could chat, to whom he could let down his hair, in whom he could confide. So it was good that Anna would be with him. And finally, in part I am sure to put salve on some of the hurt of my disappointment, Harry asked me to have dinner with him. He wanted, he said, to talk over with me some of the things he had on his mind before he left to meet Father at Malta. About that time I realized that I was allowing myself to be a little childish about the whole thing, and instantly began to cheer up.

And over dinner at his quarters Harry did what he was so good at: he was a charming and interesting companion, flashing with ideas and with wit, and we had a very good time. He put it down as his prediction, having talked earlier with Ike Eisenhower, that all Nazi resistance would have crumbled by July. I scoffed, and bet him it would be no later than the end of April. He told me that Churchill had another southern invasion up his sleeve: what the P.M. referred to as a diversion in the North Adriatic, to break the Italian stalemate. We smiled over this latest effort to get Allied soldiers into the Balkans ahead of the Russians, and Harry announced confidently that the American Joint Chiefs would never permit landing-craft desperately needed in the Pacific to be used for the P.M.'s purpose.

He said Father was sure that this Crimean meeting would be the last Big Three conference necessary before the end of the war. The agenda for the meeting was to be almost entirely devoted to the structure of the peace, the organization of the United Nations, the problems of control and government in the various countries of Europe and Asia, which would, in the absence of such plans, find themselves in an administrative vacuum.

And, pursued Harry, Father was insistent that Stalin and Churchill and he have a specific meeting of minds on the machinery of the peace, so that from the first moment after hostilities ceased the conquered nations would start learning the lessons of their crimes. Father was anxious, he said, to make sure that when the Nazis were licked, and our military government in charge, the officers in command not be one-time corporation big-shots, whose only interest would be in building up Germany's cartels all over again.

I finished dinner in good spirits. Harry was scheduled to leave next day for Rome, where he had appointments at the Vatican before he would proceed to Malta to join Father. I gave him messages to take to Father, thanked him for his thoughtfulness, and headed back to my job.

So—no Yalta for me. More important, I never again saw Father alive.

10

YALTA CONFERENCE

DESPITE THE FACT that I was not Father's companion at Malta, nor in the days of the conference at Yalta, nor later at Great Bitter Lake in Egypt, I was in a position to get more than one first-hand account of what happened at those places. One set of impressions I received later from my sister Anna; from Harry Hopkins I received another. And Father had time to send me some letters in which he gave me some of his personal reactions. From these different—and individual—accounts, which all tally in the major particulars, and with the help of the official log of the trip, I have been able to form this picture:

The Crimean Conference, with its way-stops at Malta and in Egypt, was the longest in point of time (Father was away from the United States for some five weeks); it permitted of more conversations between the leaders of the Big Three (there were eight formal meetings and many other informal talks during the eight days Father was in the Crimea, and they covered the full spectrum of military and political questions); but, nevertheless, it was not the war's most important high-level conference.

The principal reason for this was that, in the main, the decisions had been taken elsewhere—in Washington, in Cairo, in Teheran. At Yalta the Soviet Marshal, the British Prime Minister, and the American President, together with their military and diplomatic aides, had as their job to fill in the specifics of the general agreement they had already come to. More advisers than ever before had to attend. And there can be no question of the importance of many of these details. But the overall picture had been projected at Teheran. If Father had lived, there would unquestionably have been other Big Three meetings than simply the one at Potsdam. Yalta was necessary because the broad policy laid down at Teheran had not been smoothly put into effect at Dumbarton Oaks; one level below the Big Three the representatives of the three countries were not seeing eye to eye. At Yalta, once again, there was unanimity, and the flesh was put on the skeleton of the postwar world. That is its importance.

It was held in the Crimea for the convenience of Stalin, whose Red Army had begun its expected winter offensive a week or so before Father left Washington. It had been reported, indeed, that this offensive was launched a week earlier than first planned, and in spite of bad weather, in order to relieve the last pressure the Nazis were bringing on the Allied troops in the west.

The P.M. had not been at all happy about the choice of Yalta for the conference: Harry Hopkins reported Churchill's reaction to Father.

"He says that if we had spent ten years on research we

could not have found a worse place in the world than Yalta. . . . He claims it is good for typhus and deadly lice which thrive in those parts." A day or so later the P.M. sent a message himself, claiming that the automobile drive from the airfield at Saki to Yalta took six hours and that part of the road which led over and through the mountains was at best frightening and at worst impassable; that finally the Germans had left the whole countryside in such dreadful condition that the health of the conferees would be in definite jeopardy.

The contents of the P.M.'s notes were noted, and filed away. And at Malta, when Father got there on February 2nd and was met by Averell Harriman, he learned that the drive would be okay and that health conditions would be okay. That was that.

The first military staff conferences were held at Malta. As some indication of the success of Allied arms, it can be set down that the only real point of issue, as far as the Joint Chiefs were concerned, was what part of our strength should remain applied in the European theater, how much added to the Pacific theater. Admiral King and the Navy officers, who for quite obvious reasons had always taken more interest in the war against the Japanese, were now—if rather mildly—opposed to General Marshall's conviction that all possible force should be brought to bear in Europe so as to finish off the Nazis in the quickest possible time. The Combined Chiefs had been in session for the past several days in Malta: the two appointments they had with Father and the one with Churchill were to report the solution of what minor differences had existed among them.

And there was time, too, for Father and Anna to take a thirty-mile ride around Malta, in the pleasant, warm sunshine, and to see the stone replica of the scroll which he had presented to the people of Malta on his last visit.

The fourteen-hundred mile flight to the Crimea began that night. All night, one every ten or fifteen minutes, the big C-54's roared up from Luqa airfield, bound east to the southern tip of Greece, then northeast up over the Aegean Sea and the Black Sea to Saki, while underneath their airborne path American and Soviet warships cruised, insurance against the possibility of a forced landing.

In Plane Number 1, Father's plane, Leahy, McIntire, and Brown, Pa Watson, Mike Reilly, and Arthur Prettyman watched the six fighter planes that picked them up at Athens, and the one that turned back with engine trouble. Noon, and Father's plane was landing on Soviet soil, to be met by Molotov, Secretary of State Stettinius, and Averell Harriman. Twenty minutes later the P.M.'s plane put down, and honors were rendered them together by a Red Army band and a company of Red Army honor guards. *The Star-Spangled Banner, God Save the King,* the *Internationale,* and then Anna and Father were in a Russian limousine, with a Russian driver, speeding first over rolling, snow-covered country, and later winding high up to the Red Crag. From Saki to Yalta the roadway was guarded by Soviet troops. And Anna tugged at Father's sleeve.

"Look! How many of them are girls!"

At Livadia Palace, once the Czar's summer palace, then a rest-home for tubercular citizens, then staff headquarters for the Nazi marauders, the caravan of cars carrying the American party pulled up. The Nazis had left nothing, when they were driven from Livadia Palace —nothing but two small pictures, which had been hung on a wall of Father's bedroom. But the Russians had brought from Moscow a complete hotel staff and furnishings as appropriate as it had been possible to lay hands on. And Harriman's daughter Kathleen was on hand, too, to welcome them. They were all exhausted: their schedule was bath, dinner, and bed—General Marshall in what had been the Imperial bedroom, Admiral King in what had been the Czarina's boudoir.

Twelve miles away was the villa set aside for use by the P.M.; six miles away was Stalin's villa. The Marshal arrived early the next morning, a Sunday; by four o'clock that afternoon he and Molotov had made their first informal call on Father; by five the conference was hard at work, in the first formal meeting around the great round table in Livadia's grand ballroom. It lasted two hours and forty minutes, and it set the tone for the seven meetings that followed, one a day. Only the last meeting was shorter. There was a lot of work:

1. The completely unified details of the war on Hitlerism. And while the conferences were going on, the Red Army was chewing up Nazis at an unprecedented rate. Indeed, there was speculation on the part of the British and the American military and naval delegates whether the Russians had not irrevocably broken the German lines in the east, and the collapse of the world's most powerful fascist state might not take place even before the conference was adjourned.

2. The occupation and control of Germany, after her defeat. Father had come to the Crimea hoping to convince the other partners that control of Germany should be integrated, not divided into zones. That control and administration should be joint not only at the top, but all the way down the line. But both the British and the Soviets were lukewarm to the idea; they were able to convince Father that the zone idea should be set up; at Yalta the lines of demarcation were settled and agreed upon, and the time at which the different armies should set up administrative control each in its own zone was likewise settled.

"It is our inflexible purpose," wrote the three partners, "to destroy German militarism and Nazism and to ensure that Germany will never again be able to disturb the peace of the world. We are determined . . . to eliminate or control all German industry. . . ." Father was a proponent of what was known in this country as the Morgenthau plan, the terms of which called for striking at the heart of the industrial potential without which no modern nation can wage war. He found a ready listener to this plan in Marshal Stalin. It is the fault of neither of these two men that these stringent terms have not been followed out.

3. Reparation by Germany was likewise determined, and a schedule—including dates of delivery and character of reparations, industrial equipment and the like—established. (This schedule has not been followed by the British or by the Americans.)

4. A United Nations Conference, the foundations of which were laid at Dumbarton Oaks, having been pre-

viously agreed upon in large at Teheran, was called for San Francisco, less than two months in the future. The stumbling block at Dumbarton Oaks had been a question of voting procedure: should the veto by one of the Big Three be permitted to halt action by a Security Council of the United Nations—action against any country accused of aggression, for example?

At Yalta the partners look this problem squarely in the eye—and on the level it required. Both Father and Stalin approved the concept of the veto power for the Big Three, basing their arguments on the simple, crystal-clear fact that if the peace is to be maintained it can be maintained only if all the world's greatest powers concur. If two of them fall out with the third, if one falls out with the other two, the peace is in danger. Only unity and integrity of purpose can save the peace.

The solution of the dilemma posed by this procedural question was Father's. The Big Three, plus China and France, must agree unanimously, so said the solution, before the world organization can take economic or military action against an aggressor. But any seven of the Security Council's eleven members can cite an aggressor nation and call it to account before the tribunal of world opinion.

Father was categorically insistent on the need for maintaining the utmost integrity among the nations, and especially among the Big Three. And this approach to the veto principle preserved that integrity.

5. The Three answered the questions posed by the liberation of European countries—and in doing so reaffirmed the principles of the Atlantic Charter.

This meant self-government, this meant the right of all peoples to choose their own form of government, this meant free elections.

6. With respect to Poland, Stalin insisted on the Curzon Line—with minor revisions in favor of the Poles—as that country's eastern boundary, and in the same breath plumped for keeping Poland a strong and self-sufficient nation by adding to its territory in the north and west, at the expense of conquered Germany. A compromise had to be reached in the establishment of a government for Poland which would be in fact a government of national unity: the Russians had a Polish government in Moscow, the British backed the old Polish government operating out of London. Father's rôle was mediator and arbitrator—as it was so important for unity that it continue to be.

7. Churchill, jealous of British interests in the Mediterranean and the Balkan countries particularly, insisted on a review of Yugoslavia's future: it was agreed that a temporary parliament would include members of the last Yugoslav parliament, but, at Stalin's behest, only such as had not compromised themselves "by collaboration with the enemy."

8. Father was convinced that frequent meetings of the Big Three were an urgent need: this conference in the Crimea, held only slightly more than a year after that at Teheran, was proof. So a regular and continuing schedule of meetings of the three foreign secretaries was set up.

9. Wisely, solemnly, and truly, the Three set it down

as their belief that: "Only with the continuing and growing cooperation and understanding among our three countries and among all the peace-loving nations can . . . be realized a secure and lasting peace. . . ." The first word of that quotation deserves attention. So does the number: Three.

Harry Hopkins is my witness for the statement that the unity of Churchill, Stalin, and Roosevelt was a firmer and more tangible thing at Yalta than at Teheran. And it was evident that Father's rôle, even more than at earlier conferences, was that of leader. It is not by chance that he sat in the middle, when the pictures were taken. He dominated Winston Churchill more completely than before; Joseph Stalin was likewise prepared to heed Father's counsel, to accept Father's solutions.

And there was at Yalta, perhaps even more than at the earlier conferences, a sense of the tremendous and encompassing responsibility which was on those three pairs of shoulders. There were differences, on all levels; there were differences even within the various delegations themselves—Father, for example, was not prepared to trust implicitly all his advisers. But all these differences were submerged in the face of the awesome task of building a sure, strong peace.

And there were revealing incidents, too.

There was the time, at a dinner in Stalin's villa, when Father—diplomatically, but sincerely, too—praised the Soviet champagne, and was proudly informed by his host that it came from Stalin's own homeland, Georgia. And Father made the proud smiles deeper by volunteering that after the war, when he was no longer President, he would like the opportunity of getting rich by selling that champagne in America, on commission.

And there was the Soviet stroke of diplomacy, in their drawing attention to the fact that the weather in the Crimea had been unpleasant up until the moment of Father's arrival. They knew the legend: it was the Soviets who put their tongues, in describing it, to the phrase "Roosevelt weather."

There were exchanges of presents, and of honors: from Father to the P.M., to Stalin, to Eden, and to Molotov went specially engraved medallions; from Father to Stalin went, also, a copy of the book *Target: Germany*, perhaps as a mildly politicalized hint as to the weight of the Allied POINTBLANK, code word for the all-out bombing of strategic areas in Germany. And Father, too, presented to the Marshal eight decorations—two, Legion of Merit, degree of chief commander; six, Legion of Merit, degree of commander—for Stalin to give to eight Red Army officers.

And as the American party left Livadia, on Sunday, February 11th, the Soviet staff at the palace pressed on them vodka, several kinds of Russian wines, the Georgian champagne Father had complimented, caviar, butter, oranges, and tangerines. Which reminded my sister Anna that one morning, when she had been out for a walk in company with an English-speaking Soviet secret service agent, she had come on a group of Russian children and given them bars of chocolate. The children had accepted them but the secret service agent had gravely and firmly handed back the chocolate with the words:

"They have enough food. We do not wish the American lady to think that they lack."

But before the conference broke up, Stalin had once more given the assurance he had first volunteered in Teheran: that within six months of V-E Day, the Soviets would have declared war on Japan; then, pausing in thought, he had revised that estimate from six months to three months.

And, in addition to the points covered in the official statement, the Big Three were agreed that Soviet security in Pacific waters involved their title to the Kurile Islands, as well as to the southern half of Sakhalin. Later, when the criticism over "secret deals" was leveled at Father and his partners because of this agreement, what the critics evidently chose to overlook was the fact that the arrangement could not possibly be made public, in the light of Russia's then non-involvement in the war against Japan. Nor is it accurate to say that the Kuriles were Russia's "price" for entry into the war against Japan, for Stalin had volunteered the step more than a year before, in Teheran, with no thought of "payment."

The drive from Livadia brought Father to Sevastopol at dusk, perhaps the best time to see that bleak desolation of one of the most war-devastated cities in the world. Rubble; here and there a wall standing up sheer and flat, like a billboard. Father was told there were only six buildings left standing when the Germans fled.

A night's sleep aboard the naval auxiliary USS *Catoctin*, and with the morning, the long flight to Egypt, to Deservoir Field, a thousand miles away. There the travelers found the *Quincy*, the heavy cruiser on which they had come from Newport News, waiting for them. Waiting for them, too, was the news of how the world had received their deliberations at Yalta: even Herbert Hoover had a grudging "It will offer a great hope to the world." Father glanced over some of the newspaper editorials which had been cabled to him, and then sent a bread-and-butter radiogram to Stalin, adding: "I am sure that the peoples of the world will regard the achievements of this meeting . . . as a genuine assurance that our three great nations can work as well in peace as they have in war."

There were three important visitors who called on Father, as he rested aboard the *Quincy*. Anna told me later that he was a very tired man, exhausted from the tension of the last two weeks, thin, seeming to carry on principally on nerve. But he wanted, despite his great fatigue, to meet and talk with these visitors.

First came King Farouk of Egypt, and the talk was of the long-staple Egyptian cotton America had bought during the war, of the importance of two-way trade after the war, of the thousands of Americans who, Father confidently predicted, would come flocking as tourists to the valley of the Nile. That afternoon the second of his royal visitors was piped aboard: dark Haile Selassie, the Conquering Lion of Judah, Emperor of Ethiopia. Eagerly the Emperor talked to Father of the improvements he was launching in his country, and anxiously he endorsed Father's hopes for closer relations, after the war, between the two nations.

The next morning brought the third visitor: King Ibn Saud, of Saudi Arabia, on his first trip away from his kingdom. He had come on an American destroyer, and as she was warped alongside the *Quincy,* Father's party could see the awnings that had been rigged on her decks, so that the King could sleep out-of-doors. Discreetly, my sister Anna had taken her leave of Father that day for a trip to Cairo, out of deference for the Moslem custom of secluding the women of the family.

The King and the President talked first of the Jewish question in Palestine. It had been Father's hope that he would be able to convince Ibn Saud on the equity of the settlement in Palestine of the tens of thousands of Jews driven from their European homes, persecuted, wandering. Later Bernard Baruch was to tell me that Father had confessed that of all the men he had talked to in his life, he had got least satisfaction from this iron-willed Arab monarch. Father ended by promising Ibn Saud that he would sanction no American move hostile to the Arab people.

Of Syria and the Lebanon, French colonies inhabited importantly by Arabs, Father told his visitor that he had in writing the guarantee of the French government that Syria and the Lebanon would be granted their independence. He assured him that he could at any time write to the French government insisting that they honor their word, and that he would back up the Lebanese and the Syrians with all possible support short of the use of force.

And Ibn Saud, looking enviously at Father's wheelchair, was surprised when Father promptly made him a present of it.

Then up the Suez Canal to the Mediterranean, and the

first leg of the long voyage home. At Algiers there was a short halt, while waiting for an answer to the question: Would de Gaulle hold his sulk? Or would he deign to pay Father a visit, as he had been invited to do? And the answer, via Ambassador Caffery: "For a list of reasons de Gaulle cannot leave Paris at this juncture. Unfortunately. Algiers is far away, etcetera, etcetera." So Father shrugged, and the *Quincy* got under way for Newport News.

For a return from such a successful and eventful conference, the trip home was a sad one. One of Father's oldest and closest friends, Pa Watson, had suffered an attack on the way west from Alexandria; halfway across the Atlantic he died. It was little wonder, Anna reported to me later, that Father was so mortally tired when he reached the White House.

And yet, he could say with a return of his old warmth, to Mother, when they were reunited:

"Look at the communiqué from the Crimea: the path it charts! From Yalta to Moscow, to San Francisco and Mexico City, to London and Washington and Paris! Not to forget it mentions Berlin!

"It's been a global war, and we've already started making it a global peace!"

11

CONCLUSION

THE JOB OF FORGING a global peace was begun, and well begun. Somewhere, at some point in the months since Franklin Roosevelt's death, his brave beginning has been prejudiced. It may be that "prejudiced" is too mild a word. It may be that it should read: The peace is fast being lost.

The evidence of the truth of this sober statement is at every hand. "There is no peace," cries Walter Lippmann; the newspapers print stories of advanced air bases in the extreme eastern section of our administrative zone in Germany, and tell of how our air forces there are being built up, with the latest, speediest rocket planes replacing the "antiquated" P-51's. The question cries for an answer: Why?

Or think of the suspicion bred by our jealous and insane reluctance to share the "secret" of the atom bomb, a "secret" which every scientist who worked on the Manhattan Project declares flatly is no secret whatever. Yet we hug to our bosom, safe from our "untrustworthy" allies, this murderous toy, and give it over rather to the control of men in Army uniform, just as though we were a militarist state and not, thanks to our Founding Fathers, a civilian democracy.

The evidence can be multiplied as easily as breathing.

Our job is to find out the underlying causes, why it is that the peace is fast being lost, why it is that the knowledgeable gossip at Washington cocktail parties is of war with the Soviet Union "preferably before 1948"—which is to say, preferably before the Soviets can perfect *their* version of an atomic weapon. Why can correspondents write, "Every statesman in Europe has it in the back of his mind as his ultimate controlling assumption that he must act as if there were going to be a war between Britain and Russia, which will involve all the other nations?" We must find out who these statesmen are; we must attack their controlling assumption; we must fight for the global peace which seemed so sure when V-J Day followed V-E Day.

And the job begins by figuring out: What change was there, which swerved us from the road to peace and has sent us pell-mell in the opposite direction?

I believe that there is one fact which, once grasped and understood, leads to clarity and appreciation of all postwar political facts. This one fact is that when Franklin Roosevelt died, the force for progress in the modern world lost its most influential and most persuasive advocate. With his death, the most articulate voice for integrity among the nations and the peoples of the world was stilled. More than that, for people everywhere in the world, he had been the symbol of America, and of freedom, on whom they had pinned their hope of liberation and a new world of peace and plenty; when he died, some of their hope died with him, and their faith.

Now it must be obvious that no single individual, no matter how great a world leader, can by his existence or by his death influence world history for more than a few moments of eternity. But in this case, an individual's death meant a consequent vacuum—for those few moments—in the force for progress, for moving forward, for making sure that the war was not fought, after all, just to preserve the *status quo ante*. And into the vacuum, the friends of progress being out to lunch, there stepped their opposites, the foes of progress, the proponents of the world that *was*, the advocates of reaction.

It is not hard to cite specific exhibits to warrant this thesis. In the earlier pages of this book I have set down, from my personal knowledge, many of the plans which the architect of our global victory discussed with other leaders. In them there is the promise. Place the promise next to the performance, and what do we find?

There is the instance of China. At Cairo, Franklin Roosevelt wrung a promise from the feudal warlord who happened also to be the *de facto* war leader of China. The promise was that *before the cessation of hostilities* a truly representative government of China's national unity would be formed, and that under the aegis of this new and more democratic government there would then —as promptly as possible—be held national elections. True, it was a conditional promise. Chiang's conditions were two: first, that Father should obtain from the Soviet government full assurance that Manchuria would be returned to Chinese sovereignty and full assurance that the future Chinese boundary would be respected, this commitment to include an understanding that the Soviets would not interfere in China's internal political problems; second, that the United States should back the Chinese in their postwar refusal of extraterritorial rights to the British in Hong Kong, Canton, and Shanghai, and as a sort of emphasis laid on this condition Chiang was told that only American warships would enter those and other Chinese ports and that British warships would be excluded when Japanese resistance ceased.

The performance? Father's special envoy, Pat Hurley, did a remarkable job. All the necessary assurances were received from the Soviets, who in fact have lived up to the letter and spirit of their agreement since that time. It then devolved on the United States to fulfill *its* conditional responsibility. We did not. The first warships to enter Chinese ports were British warships. The order excluding them was "held up" somewhere, in all probability in the State Department.

The result? Faced with a broken American promise, Chiang in turn broke his. The picture today in China is not one of progress, but of continuing reaction. The Government is not a government of national unity, with all parties represented, but a government of despotism with famine at the bottom and bribes and cynicism at the top.

A comparison of promise and performance in the colonial world evidences a still sharper disparity. Take the Dutch East Indies, concerning which Queen Wilhelmina had said she would announce *immediately on the cessa-*

tion of hostilities that they would first have dominion status with later a swift opportunity to vote themselves independence. True, this commitment had been made on the understanding that it would be American troops which would liberate those rich colonies. In fact, as the world noted with dismay, the British—mindful of the effects of Javanese independence on their own colonial peoples—shot into the Dutch East Indies as though out of a gun and used American Lend-Lease material to suppress most ruthlessly the struggle of those peoples for independence, while in America we did—precisely nothing.

Or take French Indo-China. How often Father maintained that this colony, liberated in main part by American arms and American troops, should never be simply handed back to the French, to be milked by their imperialists as had been the case for decades! Yet, when British colonial troops marched in, they took with them French troops and French administrators. Quick! While the time is ripe! Give it back to the same imperialist interests, while no one is looking!

But these instances, important and indicative as they are, are nevertheless only knee-high to the most serious evidence that progress has been superseded by reaction. This exhibit is the breakdown of the unity of the Big Three, a unity which is the keystone of the peace. Franklin Roosevelt chiseled that keystone and set it in place; a great many men have since been chipping away at it, hoping that it will next moment crumble.

These saboteurs of international unity are headed by the men who insist that the principle of the veto power is wrong. These are the men who either through ignorance or cupidity blink the fact that in a world dominated by three powers, the U.S.A., the U.S.S.R., and the U.K., *all three* must work in concert if the peace is to be maintained. Nor is it enough to contend that the Soviets are so stubborn and so greedy that *no* self-respecting power can maintain unity with them, without—horrid word!—appeasing them. This argument won't wash, for the world has seen the fact of Big Three unity; noted it approvingly for many, many months; noted it, in fact, on through the time of the Foreign Ministers' conference at Moscow in December, 1945-January, 1946. It was only *after* that conference, when in this country a great hue-and-cry was set up that Byrnes had sold the United States down the river, when under the verbal leadership of men like Vandenberg in the Senate and the Hearst-Roy Howard-McCormick chorus in our press there was a call for "get-tough-with-Russia"—only then did our unity worsen.

And what was the terrible thing that Byrnes had done at Moscow? He had discussed the possibility of eventually placing the atom bomb under United Nations control. For Byrnes was clear-eyed enough to realize that if there was one single factor magnificently calculated to breed suspicion of rich, powerful America in the minds and hearts of the countries who were our Allies in war and presumably our allies for peace, it was that we were concealing the world's most devastating weapon. Why? For use against whom?

Well, apparently Byrnes learned his lesson. Two months later he had listened to some inner voice, and was ready to promulgate his own brand of the "get-tough-with-Russia" line. By a curious happenstance, it was only one week later that Winston Churchill, who had fought an unceasing battle to avoid a cross-channel invasion into Europe—from the spring of 1942 until the winter of 1943-44—who had constantly struggled to force a change in Allied strategy so that our troops would be called on to penetrate the mountain barriers which he called with a straight face the "soft underbelly of Europe," made his speech at Fulton, Missouri, in which he directed a savage onslaught against the Soviets. He had tried to shift the weight of the offensive so as to protect British Empire interests in the Balkans and central Europe against his Soviet ally and to the jeopardy of swift victory; now he was busy running up a trial balloon for outright war against his former ally. Nor could he have been unaware, at the time he suggested an Anglo-American military alliance, that the Combined Chiefs of Staff were still meeting regularly in Washington, long months after the "end" of the war—*as they are still meeting.*

The gradual breakdown of the desperately needed Big Three unity in fact can be dated as beginning even before the war's end. Three months before the Nazi collapse, the Foreign Ministers and the War Ministers of the Big Three began to circulate, between London, Washington, and Moscow, draft memoranda of what the surrender terms should be. After some discussion, there was final agreement on this document. A copy was forwarded from Moscow to Marshal Zhukov. No copy was forwarded, either from London or Washington, to General Eisenhower at SHAEF. In fact the surrender terms he used were drawn up by his Chief of Staff, General

Beedle Smith, for the reason that he knew of no existing document. Is it any wonder that the Soviets were miffed? Or that later they resented American and British troops not withdrawing promptly to the occupation zones which had been agreed upon at Yalta? Or that at this writing they are quite properly aggrieved that British and American occupation forces are making no particular effort to fulfill the reparations schedules likewise established at Yalta?

As these things occurred, they inevitably produced a reaction in the Kremlin. Undoubtedly, from V-E Day forward, Stalin and his advisers determined that if the overall picture of Allied disunity was going to be so marked, they would promptly start thinking of mending their wall, against any eventuality. Iron curtains do not simply grow. There are reasons for their existence. If a Churchill could talk about an iron curtain in Europe, a Stalin could point to the reasons for its necessity. Unfortunately, international politics being what they are, logic is replaced by the "You're another!" technique. In my effort to get back to first and underlying causes for our critical present, I note only that it was the United States and Great Britain who first shook the mailed fist, who first abrogated the collective decisions.

And it should be noted, too, that in the world shakedown that followed the end of the shooting, we vacated the vitally important rôle of operating as mediator between Great Britain and the Soviet Union, the only two nations whose security interests clash today. Rather than arbitrating those differences, as Father had always been careful to do, we chose sides; worse than that, we did not simply line up *beside* Britain, we lined up *in back of* her. Thus, in the tragic case of Greece, where British soldiers, despite an outspoken protest on the part of the British people, cold-bloodedly shot down Greek anti-fascists, we took the part of the British Foreign Office in declaring that mockery of an election truly democratic; likewise, in Turkey we supported British aims in chivvying a none-too-reluctant Turkey into the position of opposing any Soviet ambitions toward joint control of the Dardanelles. Two nations control the Dardanelles, geographically: Greece and Turkey. By supporting the British when they impose anti-Soviet conditions on that critically important waterway, we once again negate the principle of Big Three unity.

Or there is the case of Iran. Here would be high comedy, if it were not at the same time laden with bitterness. The Security Council of the United Nations—often with complete disregard for the wishes of the Iranian government—insisted, as a result of British and American leadership, on keeping the case of Iran alive just as though it ever represented any serious threat to the peace. The facts were easily arrived at: Great Britain was jealously guarding its control of oil concessions in southern Iran, on a fifty-one to forty-nine basis—the lion's share going of course to the British lion. When the Soviet Union presumed to dicker on a fifty-fifty basis for the northern oil concessions (and remember how close Iran is to the Soviet's Baku oilfields), the UN's Security Council made of the affair an anti-Soviet field day. All over the United States there was such general agreement on the part of columnists and commentators that the Russians were imperialistic that we who read and listened were almost ready to accept the distortion simply because it had been so often repeated.

Iran is only important as it is indicative—indicative that a small group of willful men in London and Washington are anxious to create and foster an atmosphere of war hatred against the Russians, just as though the Russian people had not borne the brunt of the military force of Nazism, borne it, overthrown it, and thereby demonstrated for all time their importance to the coalition for peace.

If I speak with such emphasis, it is because I have, in very small part, earned the right to do so, by virtue of having worked with and flown with more men who have died than I like to remember. And it is not pleasant to realize that what they did is being disregarded, so very few months later, and by individuals who were never to be found in the right corner, even after Pearl Harbor. It is not pleasant to realize that the voice of the new "internationalist" is the most strident today—the Congressman whose idea of internationalism is an international combination to bring about a World War III against one of our World War II allies.

I have used the phrase "a small group of willful men," and I have placed them in Washington. Perhaps I should be even more specific. I am thinking of the career men in the State Department whom Father never trusted, including certain men often mistakenly referred to as our "experts" on foreign affairs. I am thinking of the reactionaries of both major parties in Congress, men who have decided that it is more important to choose up sides for the future than it is to work together for the future. I am thinking of our guardians of the "free press"—the press that heroically contends for freedom of irresponsibility. These are the most vituperative voices lifted against the principle of Big Three unity, as a result of their insistence that the veto power is a "vicious system."

And I am thinking, too, of the men who have shrunk our foreign policy down to the size of the atom bomb, the Army officers who—considering apparently only their professional futures—are prepared out-of-hand to condemn civilization to a heap of rubble.

I have voiced my thankful opinion that American custom and tradition dictates that the military shall not control the destiny of the nation. It was, I am sure, by no coincidence that it was stipulated that the President—traditionally a civilian—should be Commander-in-Chief of the Army and Navy. Yet we must reflect soberly on the fact that the military have taken over the task of postwar diplomacy. I make no criticism of General Marshall's work in the Orient. Nor do I single out General Beedle Smith, in Moscow. Nor do I contend that Admiral Leahy is not the best adviser a President ever had on diplomatic affairs. But I will argue that such important diplomatic posts should be given over to civilians, that it is not appropriate for a non-warrior democracy like the United States of America to depend on brass and braid for information and guidance in international affairs. Military personalities who enter the arena of American politics or foreign service should completely sever themselves from the armed forces and retire first to civilian life.

The danger of a military diplomacy must be obvious; the military commands the Army, and an army will be a force for progress only as it is the instrument for a progressive foreign policy. That is why, no matter how competent or how high-minded they may be, no men should be in the position of controlling both foreign policy and the Armed Forces. The attitude of our troops abroad bears interesting witness to this thesis. So long as our GI's were convinced they were involved in winning a war, in the main they cheerfully and with remarkably few beefs forewent the pleasure and comfort of home and wife and children for the responsibility of fighting and winning. The GI "let's-go-home" riots did not take place even as late as Potsdam, when there still seemed to be—and was—a definite job for democracy to do in running a conquered nest of fascism. But just so soon as it became obvious that the things for which they had fought—principally the "peace for many generations" assured the world by the concord of the Big Three at Teheran—were going by the board, the howl that went up from Paris to Tokyo was registered quite sensitively in Washington.

Let me make it very clear that I am not opposed to maintaining a large group of Americans under arms. On the contrary, I am in favor of it—*if that army is to be used as part of the security force stipulated by the United Nations charter, and if the United Nations proceed from the assumption which was their foundation,* which is to say, the ever-closer unity of the Big Three.

I have come to the question: What can *we* do, we who are not simply officials in the American government but something far more important, which is to say, American citizens? What can we do to ensure our Government's return to the path that was charted by Franklin Roosevelt?

To answer this question, I must set down, very briefly, a lesson that was taught me first by history and later by observation of my father as President. Those Presidents of our country were greatest, I am convinced, who were most sensitive and most responsive to the informed and intelligent will of the people. Lincoln could not sign the Emancipation Act, freeing the slaves, until nearly two years after the Civil War had begun, not because there was not pressure from the North that he do so, but because there was not sufficient pressure. There is a relationship, in an American democracy, between their President and the people, which only too rarely is what it should be. We who are sovereign, we who are American citizens, must help if any President is to be a great President. If Franklin Roosevelt was a great President, it was—in the main—thanks to the articulated intelligence of the American people during his terms in the White House.

INDEX